THE ART OF
CHAIR-MAKING

▲▽▲▽▲▽▲▽▲▽▲▽▲

Kerry Pierce

Sterling Publishing Co., Inc.
New York

Chapter Ten has previously appeared in a different form in "Woodwork" magazine. A variation of Chapter Seven appeared in "Woodshop News."

Library of Congress Cataloging-in-Publication Data
Pierce, Kerry.
    The art of chair-making / Kerry Pierce.
       p. cm.
    Includes index
    ISBN 0-8069-9466-5
     1. Chairs—United States 2. Furniture making—
United States I. Title.
    TT197.5.C45P54   1997
    684.1'3—dc21   97-22144
                                      CIP

Illustrations by Kevin Pierce
Book Design by Judy Morgan
Editing and Layout by R. Neumann

1 3 5 7 9 10 8 6 4 2

Published by Sterling Publishing Company, Inc.
387 Park Avenue South, New York, NY 10016
© 1997 by Kerry Pierce
Distributed in Canada by Sterling Publishing
c/o Canadian Manda Group, One Atlantic Avenue, Suite 105
Toronto, Ontario, Canada M6K 3E7
Distributed in Great Britain and Europe by Cassell PLC
Wellington House, 125 Strand, London WC2R 0BB, England
Distributed in Australia by Capricorn Link (Australia) Pty Ltd.
P.O. Box 6651, Baulkham Hills, Business Centre, NSW 2153, Australia
Printed in Hong Kong

Sterling ISBN 0-8069-9466-5

CONTENTS

▲▼▲▼▲▼▲▼▲▼▲▼▲▼▲▼▲▼▲▼▲▼▲▼▲▼▲▼▲▼▲▼▲▼▲▼▲▼

ACKNOWLEDGMENTS

▲▽▲▽▲▽▲▽▲▽▲▽▲▽▲▽▲▽▲▽▲▽▲▽▲▽▲▽▲▽

I'd like to thank the usual suspects:

Elaine, a first-rate wife and mom, who somehow manages to keep our home functioning smoothly.

Em, a first-rate daughter and my softball hero.

Andy, who is not only a first-rate son, but who is also—as can be seen in the photo of the one-board swing—a first-rate model.

My brother, Kevin, who labored long and hard to prepare the measured drawings.

All those chair-makers who were kind enough to share photos of their work for the gallery section: Curtis Buchanan, Owen Rein, David Wright, William Locke, and Brian Boggs. All are gifted craftsmen.

Joe Graham, who not only shared photos of his chairs, but who also read over some of the technical matter.

And Verne, too.

PREFACE

▲▽▲▽▲▽▲▽▲▽▲▽▲▽▲▽▲▽▲▽▲▽▲▽▲▽▲▽▲▽

The perfect American chair-making book would be written by committee.

On that committee there would be a chair-maker who specialized in accurate reproductions of eighteenth-century Windsors, as well as a chair-maker who specialized in contemporary Windsors. There would be a chair-maker who built country post-and-rung chairs, another who built Shaker-style and Shaker-inspired post-and-rung chairs. The committee would also have on it individuals who made reproductions of eighteenth-century high-style chairs (Queen Anne, Chippendale, Sheraton, Hepplewhite). Also on that committee would be individuals who made chairs with caned seats, individuals who made wicker chairs, individuals who made chairs with PVC frames, individuals who made chairs framed with lengths of willow . . . and many other individuals who make types of chairs I don't know enough about to even name.

This isn't that book. It is, instead, a book that looks at the various kinds of chairs, benches, and stools I build in my chair-making shop, many of which are based on Shaker originals.

Kerry Pierce

Chapter One
THE CHAIR

Sometimes we just need to sit. We can stand all day at our jobs. We can lie in our beds at night, but sometimes what we need is a transitional state, something more restful than standing but less acquiescent than reclining.

Chairs, benches, and stools were created to meet this need. They provide us with support so that we can take the weight of our bodies from our legs; but unlike beds—the only other furniture form intended to take that weight—chairs don't automatically encourage sleep. Instead, they make it possible for us to relax as we eat, talk, read, watch television, listen to music, or simply contemplate the course of our lives.

THE FIRST CHAIRS

The first chairs were, no doubt, whatever rocks or logs that happened to be close at hand—to the fire, to the fresh-killed beast, to the community of peers. Then, at some point, in the very distant past, we began to transform the raw materials supplied by nature into seating furniture that more closely met the needs of our bodies.

How far in the past? That's impossible to say. What we do know is that 3500 years ago, in Egypt, chair-making existed as a very sophisticated discipline. Included in the treasures of King Tutankhamen's tomb, for example, was a gilded, wooden throne that is—except for the quality of its workmanship and the rarity of its materials—very much like the chairs in which we sit today, with four legs joined by rungs, a back, a seat, and two arms.

Later, in the decorative arts of ancient Greece, there are many images of klismos chairs, especially preserved on pottery. These graceful chairs are characterized by plain saber legs and a simple back support, a form that has been echoed by many designers in more recent centuries.

Because of their rarity in all but recent history, chairs have not only provided comfort and support, they have also reflected the relative importance of individuals within groups. In medieval Europe, commoners seated themselves on rough, wooden benches. Those one step up the status ladder might also rest on benches, but these might be joiners' benches fastened together with the same techniques used for casework, then decorated with a bit of carving or turning. The lord of the house might sit in an actual chair with a stiff wooden back. Too, in the royal courts of the period, distinctions were sometimes drawn between those who sat in simple side chairs and those who sat in chairs with arms. And, of course, the finest chairs, those encrusted with the fussiest ornamentation, were reserved for royalty.

Even today, in an era of plentiful chairs, seating furniture remains symbolic of social stratification. A committee head is referred to as a chairman, or in our gender-sensitive times simply as the "chair." In colleges and universities, the ranking member of each of the academic departments is also referred to as the department chair. At the supper table, those individuals of the highest rank—mothers, fathers, guests—occupy the chairs with arms, while children occupy side chairs.

A functional chair can be made of the roughest materials. This contemporary willow chair provides very comfortable seating.

And the symbolism of the chair isn't confined to the designation of rank. Chairs are also used to mark the various stages of our lives. As toddlers, we sit in high chairs. As adults, we use conventional chairs, and when we are aged or infirm we rest in rocking chairs or wheelchairs. Too, various types of chairs have helped to define political goals. The Windsor, for example, although created first in England, was quickly transported to America, where, beginning in Philadelphia and then later in other locations, it was produced by the thousands, becoming the "Model T" of seating furniture—a chair that was perfectly expressive of the emerging American democracy.

More than any other form of furniture, chairs have entered our consciousness, not only serving to provide us with comfortable repose but also becoming metaphors for who we are as societies, as well as who we are as individuals.

THE EVOLUTION OF FORMS

Chair-making hasn't followed a single course from its beginnings in prehistory to the present. It has, instead, journeyed along a number of different routes, each plotted to arrive at the same destination: a skillful blending of comfort, beauty, and durability.

It is likely that benches and stools appeared first. Then as new concepts—a chair with back, a chair with back and arms, a chair with woven or shaped seat—emerged, the earlier, simpler forms continued to be produced, even as the new concepts took hold and evolved.

Some types—fully upholstered chairs, frame and slip-seat chairs, elaborately carved or turned post-and-rung chairs—became the chairs of the rich and mighty because of the artistry required in their production. Other forms—such as the bench, the stool, the shaved post-and-rung chair—became associated with the common man because they could be produced much more cheaply and, perhaps, also because they provided less comfortable seating.

Chair-making in the United States has evolved from the models brought here by the Europeans who first settled in America. In his book *The Fine Points of Furniture* (1950), Albert Sack describes two types of American-made chairs dating from the second half of the seventeenth century, both of which are patterned after European models. One type—Sack pictures examples made by Thomas Dennis of Ipswich, Massachusetts—is the wainscot chair made of milled lumber and decorated with elaborate carving. Although perhaps not comfortable by today's standards, in spite of

This nineteenth-century rocker exhibits several characteristics typical of hand-built country chairs. The seat is woven splint, the arms are simple cylinders, and the front posts taper from just above the seat to the underside of the arms.

their cushioned seats, these are grand chairs, which would have conferred enormous status upon their occupants. The second type is the post-and-rung chair. The Brewster chair, the Carver chair, and the slat-back chair are variations of this type. The post-and-rung chair consists of four turned or shaved posts into which a number of turned or shaved rungs are mortised. Four of these rungs constitute the seat frame, and over these four rungs a seating material is woven. This seating material can be rush (cattail leaves), splint (pounded and separated layers from wet ash or oak logs), or hickory bark. A back usually extends above the seat. This consists of either a rack of turned spindles set into the elongated back posts or horizontal slats mortised into them.

Later, the horizontal slats on the slat-back were replaced with the vertical slats of the banister-back Pilgrim chair. Many of these banister-back chairs, although seated with simple rush and likely assembled with the green-wood joinery associated with country chairs, are quite grand. The turned vases, coves, and beads are artfully conceived and skillfully executed, and the top slat is often deeply carved.

In the first quarter of the eighteenth century, a different type of chair made its appearance in American homes. Instead of a woven seat or a solid wood seat on which a separate cushion might be set, these chairs consist of a frame assembled with square mortise-and-tenon joinery into which a slip-seat is let. The slip-seat is simply a thin board onto which a cushioning material (often horse hair) is placed. The cushioning is then held in position under a layer of upholstery material (often leather) that is lapped over the edges of the board and held in place with tacks. This cushioned slip-seat is then held in place within the chair frame through the use of several woodscrews that enter the slip-seat from below after passing through the chair frame.

Slip-seat chairs tended to be more expensive than their predecessors. In part, this was because of the square of upholstery material, but an even larger factor was the nature of the chairs into which these slip-seats were let. Many of these featured Queen Anne motifs, with cabriole legs and spoon or drake feet (later ball-and-claw feet). They often also were decorated with leaf or shell carvings on the knees and crest rails. The manufacture of such chairs using only hand processes was both labor- and skill-intensive.

TRANSLATION TO AMERICA

Early in the eighteenth century, George III, ruler of England, was fox hunting when a terrible storm drove him to seek refuge in the home of a wheelwright. There, as he waited for the storm to pass, the king rested on a chair made of a plank seat into which four turned legs and a number of back spindles were mortised. He found the chair to be such an agreeable concoction that he ordered his cabinetmaker to build similar chairs for the royal residence at Windsor.

This story, or some variation of this story, is widely told both to account for the Windsor name and to establish the chair's pedigree. True or not,

The finial on this rocker (chair pictured in previous photo) suggests that it might have been built in one of the western Shaker communities.

the story does accurately place the location in which Windsors first appeared on the English landscape. Unlike later American examples, English Windsors tend to mimic the details of the heavier joiners' chairs that preceded them. Often standing on cabriole legs and adorned with a pierced and carved central back splat, these Windsors can be relatively grand pieces of seating furniture.

However, when the Windsor crossed the Atlantic and became Americanized, it changed in much the same way as did other transplanted furniture forms of the period. Ornament was stripped away. The chair's forms became simpler and, as carving was replaced by turned detail, less labor-intensive to build.

This simplification didn't necessarily mean crudity—although there are crude examples from the period. In the finer chairs, it meant, instead, a spare

Shaker production chairs were built at the Mt. Lebanon, New York, community. This petite rocker is typical of the chairs produced there. Notice the crisply turned acorn finials and the graceful profile of the back slats.

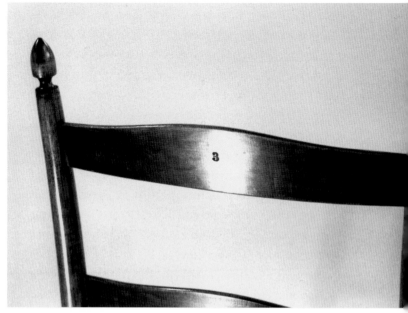

The number stamped on the back of the top slat (chair pictured in previous photo) identifies this as a #3 on a scale that went from #0, the smallest, to #7, the largest.

and understated elegance. Just as the American baroque and American rococo forms of the period exhibited restrained interpretations of grander European models, the American Windsor reduced the emphasis on surface ornamentation, focusing instead on the chair's basic forms.

In the hands of the more gifted American craftsmen, the seats became more sculptural, as more material was removed from the top surface. The bottom surface, too, was relieved, often meeting the top surface in a sharply defined line that swept dramatically around the seat. The comb (back) of the chair was elongated, the spindles attenuated, taking full advantage of the strength implicit in split and shaved stock.

In much the same way that the Shakers invigorated the post-and-rung chair during the nineteenth century, American Windsor chair-makers of the eighteenth century invigorated the Windsor by moving away from the more stately English models, reducing the chair to its most essential and its most elegant shapes.

THE SHAKER AESTHETIC

In 1774 a small group of rebellious Quakers set sail from Liverpool, England, for America. They were led by Mother Ann Lee, an uneducated millhand who had received revelations indicating that their beliefs would flourish in this country. First in Watervliet, near Albany, New York, then in other places scattered across the eastern half of the United States, they established colonies based upon piety, communal living, celibacy, and hard work.

These were the Shakers, and for much of the nineteenth century, through a combination of artful design, skillful execution, and aggressive marketing, they dominated American chair-making like no group before or since. Their brand of chair-making didn't spring fully formed from the rocky New England soil. It was, instead, a part of the already established post-and-rung tradition that reached back two hundred years to the Pilgrims.

In fact, because the first Shakers involved in this enterprise were simply converts who brought with them the knowledge and tools required for country chair-making, the earliest of the Shaker chairs (1789–1815) were indistinguishable from those made by non-Shakers. However, in the first quarter of the nineteenth century, the Shakers of several communities began producing more chairs than they needed for their own use, creating a surplus that could be offered for sale to the outside world. John Kassay (in *The Book of Shaker Furniture*), among others, identifies this period, ending in the mid-1860s, as the time in which the finest Shaker chairs were produced.

During this period, Shaker chairs began to assume their signature features. Posts were elongated. Finials were refined. Rungs became more delicate, tapering from the middle to a thin shoulder at either post. Slat and arm shapes were given more graceful curves.

The final phase of Shaker chair-making—which lasted until the closing of the Mt. Lebanon chair factory in 1935—was one of mass production. Under the direction of Robert M. Wagan (1833–1883), the chair-making operation was mechanized and streamlined. Chair sizes and shapes were standardized, and marketing became more aggressive. In the popular consciousness, the Shakers became synonymous with quality chair-making.

In the first half of this later period, the chairs that were made reflected the principles of the Shaker aesthetic. They were, although produced in grand numbers, still graceful and attractive. However, as membership in Shaker communities declined and more of the work in the Shaker chair-making operation was done by hired outsiders, and later still when many parts were contracted to companies completely outside the Shaker communities, quality declined. Rungs no longer tapered toward their shoulders, instead becoming simple dowels. Posts, too, lost their tapers, maintaining single diameters from floor to finial. Slat, arm, and finial shapes were simplified to facilitate quick production. The subtle manipulations of the elements of the Shaker chair, which had given it its spare and distinctive beauty, all but vanished, resulting in a chair that was, although unmistakably Shaker, less satisfying than its predecessors.

At the end, because of a declining male membership, the chair-making operation at Mt. Lebanon was taken over by women, the last of whom, Sister Sarah Collins, died in 1947.

In order to establish their authenticity, this decal was applied to Shaker chairs built in the Mt. Lebanon factory.

The importance of the chair-making of the Shakers did not end with the closing of the Mt. Lebanon factory or with the death of the last Shaker chair-maker. It continues today in both the specific forms being widely reproduced and in the principles of Shaker design incorporated in many modern chairs.

In his shop in Berea, Kentucky, Charles Harvey transfers measurements from a story stick to a pair of back posts for the reproduction of a Shaker chair.

A RETURN OF THE ART OF CHAIR-MAKING

In the century and a half that has passed since Shaker chair-making reached its zenith, a number of different forces have exerted themselves on American chair-making, and most, led by the Shakers' example, have been large-scale operations that all but eliminated the need for the highly skilled individual craftsman. The tens of thousands of oak chairs built in the quarter-century before World War I are typical examples. These chairs were the result of mass production, of men working not in shops but in factories.

In his introduction to John Alexander's 1978 book *Make a Chair from a Tree*, John Kelsey, then editor of "Fine Woodworking," described traditional chair-making as a "classic example of a lost art." At that time, twenty years ago, his comment was simply a statement of fact. Although, scattered across the country, there were individual craftsmen building high-quality case-pieces, chairs were another matter. These were manufactured in huge numbers by huge companies with huge machinery. And most people thought that was the way it should be. After all, people don't make chairs. Chairs are too complicated. Only factories can make chairs.

But today the situation is different. Thanks to the efforts of men like John Alexander and Michael Dunbar (*Make a Windsor with Michael Dunbar*), like Sam Maloof and Dave Sawyer, like Joe Graham and David Wright, like the dozens of American craftsmen now working at this trade in shops all over the country, chair-making has once again become a craft that individual people

Joe Graham, a chair-maker from Cleveland, Ohio, uses a flat chisel to cut a rain gutter on a Windsor chair seat.

can practice. Armed with a little knowledge, a few tools, and an interest in craftsmanship, it is possible, once again, for a single artisan to make a chair that is attractive, comfortable, and enduring.

And that is what this book is all about.

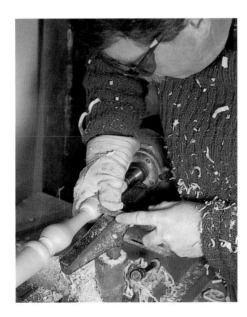

Working in a flurry of wood noodles, David Wright, of Berea, Kentucky, fashions a baluster leg for a Windsor chair.

David Wright

13

Chapter Two

MATERIALS

The classic American Windsor was built with an intimate knowledge of the properties of the various woods from which it was constructed. The seat, which was scooped out to accommodate the human bottom using only hand tools, was made of a soft, easily worked species, often white pine or poplar. Although—because of their poor resistance to breaking across the grain—these woods are unsuitable for spindles or turnings, in seat slabs of 2 or 2¼ inches, they perform admirably. The legs, which were often turned to a very complex profile of beads and coves, were made of hard maple because this species combines enormous strength with the ability to hold crisp detail. Back spindles were shaved from continuous grain ash, oak, or hickory because—even in relatively thin diameters—these woods remain strong but flexible.

Post-and-rung chairs of the eighteenth and nineteenth centuries were also built with a sensitivity to the properties of the species available to the chairmaker. Country chairs with bent back posts and bent slats were often made of oak or ash or hickory because after being treated with steam or boiling water, these species can be readily bent without breaking. The Shakers worked primarily in hard maple because this species was strong, bendable, and widely available.

The high-style frame- and slip-seat chairs of the eighteenth and nineteenth centuries (Queen Anne, Chippendale, Hepplewhite, Sheraton) were typically constructed of stock heavier in cross section than the stock used in the creation of either Windsors or post-and-rung chairs. This meant that other species, those not possessing the strength of hard maple or white oak or ash, could be used. These high-style chairs were built from the same materials used in the casework of that period. Mahogany was the wood of choice, but if mahogany wasn't available, cherry and walnut, two beautifully figured and colored native woods, were used.

The craftsmen of these earlier centuries made decisions about the suitability of particular species for particular tasks based upon a vast body of experience. Over time, they had learned that a chair post made of poplar would break easily, while one made of hard maple was all but indestructible. They had learned that a Windsor seat made of hard maple was very difficult to excavate with an adze and an inshave, but the same seat made of white pine could be quickly and efficiently shaped.

Today, however, in addition to experience, we have the advantage of scientific test data. R. Bruce Hoadley's 1980 *Understanding Wood* (and other books by other writers) is an excellent source of information on the properties of American hardwoods. The USDA Forest Products Lab in Madison, Wisconsin, is staffed with knowledgeable and cooperative men and women, as is the National Hardwood Lumber Association in Memphis, Tennessee. Contemporary chair-makers, unlike their predecessors, have the advantage of living in an age of easily accessible information on the properties of the materials with which they work

THE RIGHT CHOICE

The very first chair I ever built, a tall Windsor stool with a sculpted bicycle-style seat, was constructed of parts taken from a two-inch-thick slab of birch I'd had lying around the shop for ten or twelve years. I didn't select birch because of its suitability to the task. I selected it because it was at hand. And fortunately, although made in ignorance, the choice was a wise one, and I used that stool in my shop for almost a decade.

My first post-and-rung chair, a reproduction of a Shaker transitional rocker from the Mt. Lebanon community, was constructed of cherry. Again, my choice of material was based upon what was at hand, rather than a carefully reasoned considera-

tion of the properties of various species. In my shop at that time, I had only walnut and cherry in sufficient thicknesses to serve as post stock. I chose cherry because I preferred its color.

Again, I was fortunate. That rocker is still in use in my daughter's bedroom. However, in the years since the construction of that chair I've learned more about the physical properties of cherry—some from reference works like Hoadley's book and some from experience. Although it is a dense wood that turns and carves beautifully, cherry isn't as resistant to breaking across the grain as some other species. I don't mean it isn't suitable for chair-making—I've made almost a hundred chairs from this material without a single part failure—but shortly after the construction of that first cherry rocker, I began to beef up the parts on chairs made from this material, employing working diameters more suitable to the characteristics of this particular species.

Whereas the posts of a Shaker reproduction made of hard maple might be turned to a maximum diameter of 1⅜", the posts for the same chair made of cherry are turned to a maximum diameter of 1⁷⁄₁₆" or even 1½". The difference may seem slight, but an extra ¹⁄₁₆" of diameter adds almost 10 percent of additional wood to the post, and an extra ⅛" adds almost 20 percent of additional wood. Seat rungs, too, are strengthened. Instead of the ¹⁵⁄₁₆" diameter I often turn with hard maple or ash, when working with cherry I turn seat rungs to a sturdy 1⅛".

Having said that, I should also mention this: The maximum diameter of the posts on the cherry rocker in my daughter's room is 1¼", and the seat rungs, like the lower rungs, have a maximum diameter of ¾". Even for a chair built of hard maple or ash, these diameters would be thin, but my daughter's rocker, built of cherry, has nevertheless survived years of often vigorous rocking.

15

In large part, this survival can be attributed to the elegance of Shaker design. Unlike many country models of the same period, the durability of the classic Shaker chairs results not so much from the cross-sectional strength of any individual part; but from the collective strength of a number of tightly fit spindles running from post to post, creating a spider's web of taut engineering.

TESTING CHAIR STRENGTH

Over the years, I have built chairs that had to be rejected. In some cases, the angles at which the side rungs met the posts were wrong. In other cases, finials were misshapen. In a couple of cases, I designed chairs that were simply ugly. I hung these unseated rejects in my storage room, hoping that I would think of something that to do with them.

One day a couple of years ago, I thought of something useful: I could destroy them—not maliciously, but to gain insights into the relative strengths of chair-making woods. Although I didn't have reject chairs built from every species I've used, I did have two of cherry, one of walnut, one of ash, one of hard maple, and one of curly red maple.

I took the chairs out to the driveway of compacted stone in front of my shop. Then, grasping each by its finials, I threw it as far up into the air as I could. Some of the lighter chairs must have reached a height of fifteen or twenty feet, the heavier models a bit less. Each fell to the driveway landing crazily, sometimes on a leg or a finial, then bouncing up, careening to one side or the other, coming to rest on the back or on one of the sides.

I then gave each a careful inspection. Although they were all badly dented, none had broken apart. The only significant damage was a cracked slat on one of the cherry models.

For my second test, I again grasped each chair by its finials, and this time slammed it against the stucco-covered concrete-block wall of my shop. I cracked a couple of rungs on the cherry and curly red maple chairs, but except for some deep dents, the others were undamaged.

For my last test, I lined them up and tried to drive the heel of my work boot through the front ladder. I was able to do this with the chairs constructed of cherry and the chair constructed of curly red maple, and after several tries, I was able to break through the front ladder on the walnut chair, as well. But the chairs made of hard maple and ash resisted my best efforts. In fact, after five minutes of strenuous effort, I realized that, without tools, there was nothing I could do to cause significant damage to these chairs. In my judgment, that suggests that these woods are the best choices for chairs likely to receive very heavy loads.

CHAIR-MAKING WOODS

The list opposite includes only those species from which I have actually made chairs. Other species, available in other regions and unknown to me, will likely work as well as those listed. Consult other woodworkers and your local lumber supplier.

Hard Maple

The first choice of the nineteenth-century Shaker chair-makers, this wood possesses enormous strength, as well as the ability to hold fine-turned or carved detail. It does, however, in its nonfigured varieties, present a rather ordinary color and figure. For this reason, it is often stained or dyed.

White Ash

Like hard maple, white ash can support very heavy loads without fracturing across the grain. Because of its coarse (ring porous) nature, it's less satisfactory than some more dense species at holding fine-turned or carved detail. It is very easily bent after steaming.

Cherry

A magnificent American hardwood, cherry combines glorious color with the denseness required to hold fine-turned or carved detail. It is not, however, as suitable as some other species for chairs that will support very heavy loads.

Birch

Like hard maple, this wood is strong, dense, and—in its unfigured varieties—bland in appearance.

White Oak

Another ring-porous wood, white oak offers enormous strength. However, because of its coarse texture, it doesn't hold up well under fine-turned or carved detail. Also when worked wet, it tends to check as it dries. Like ash, it can be readily bent after steaming.

Red Oak

Although red oak is not quite as strong as white oak, this is another sturdy chair-making wood. It does not seem to check as badly as white oak when drying.

Live Oak

I've made only two chairs with this species, and I'll never make another. While a very tough wood, it's coarse and stringy under edge tools, tearing out horribly.

Red Maple

I've used only the curly variety. But at least in that form I found it very satisfactory as long as parts are beefed up a bit to compensate for its curly nature.

Walnut

Like cherry, this is a wood of breathtaking color. Also like cherry, it doesn't have quite the strength of some other species on this list.

Shagbark Hickory

Hickory is another ring-porous species and, like the ashes and the oaks, it possesses enormous strength even when turned to very fine diameters. David Wright, a Windsor chair-maker in Berea, Kentucky, makes many of his chairs from hickory, relying on its strength to permit him to turn legs to very fine diameters.

17

STANDARD LUMBER SIZES ▲▽▲▽▲▽▲▽▲▽▲▽▲▽▲▽▲▽▲▽▲▽▲▽▲▽▲▽▲▽

Boards are designated by nominal size—meaning that the stated size approximately matches the size of the rough lumber that comes directly from the sawmill. When rough lumber is planed—dressed—it is reduced to standard and uniform sizes.

Wood is also designated by quarters (of an inch). Thus a nominal one-inch-thick piece of stock is called ¼, for four quarters.

The accompanying chart relates the nominal thickness to the actual dressed dimension.

Nominal Size		Dressed
INCHES	QUARTERS	INCHES
1	⁴/₄	²⁵/₃₂
1¼	⁵/₄	1⁵/₃₂
1½	⁶/₄	1¹³/₃₂
1¾	⁷/₄	1¹⁹/₃₂
2	⁸/₄	1¹³/₁₆
2½	¹⁰/₄	2⅜
3	¹²/₄	2¾
4	¹⁶/₄	3¾

WOOD AND WATER

A fresh-cut tree produces lots of water.

How much depends on the species and the season. For example, white oak bleeds more than white ash; and any tree cut in the spring, when the sap is rising, will produce incredible amounts of water. This is because all trees are living things with powerful vascular systems that draw enormous amounts of moisture from the ground and conduct it, with the needed load of nutrients, to all the living parts of the tree. As much as 50 percent of the tree's weight is water.

If that fresh-cut tree is promptly sawn into boards, called green lumber, those boards, like the log itself, will continue to lose water, primarily through their exposed end grain but also through the sawn faces of each board.

Sometimes it's very difficult to find reasonably priced wood in the thicknesses chair-making requires. For woodworkers with access to trees one solution is cutting their own. Here Chris Sipe, owner of a portable band saw mill, and Bill Bachtel roll a shagbark hickory log onto

the loading arms of Chris's mill at a cutting site near Wadsworth, Ohio. Bill buys standing trees, fells them, and hires Chris to saw them up into usable lumber.

The band saw mill quickly transforms logs into boards.

If those boards are then stickered and allowed to dry for a summer or two, the sawn faces and the end grain will become dry to the touch. But the boards will still contain water. If they were dried outdoors in a location that allowed the free movement of air through the stack, they will have reached a state of equilibrium with the relative humidity of the surrounding air. In humid Ohio—where I live—that state of equilibrium might mean that the wood will have a July moisture content (MC) of 13 percent. Again in Ohio, during the cold, dry months of December and January, that MC on wood stored inside a heated shop might drop to 7 or even 6 percent. Then, the following summer, the MC of that wood will once again creep upward into the 12 or 13 percent range—a cycle that will repeat itself every year. And although the specific values for the MC of wood will vary from location to location due to differences in the air's relative humidity and temperature, the cycle of seasonal rising and falling MC will occur wherever lumber is cut, stored, or used.

These seasonal fluctuations are important to the woodworker because they are accompanied by corresponding dimensional changes in the wood. In general the principle can be stated this way: The greater the MC, the greater the dimensions of a particular board. The lower the MC, the smaller the dimensions of a particular board.

However, not all dimensions are changed equally by this fluctuation of MC. Lengthwise expansion and contraction is negligible—on the order of one percent—but the width and thickness of a board can vary enormously, increasing in warm, humid months, decreasing in dry, cold months. For the maker of case goods, this means that wide panels must be fastened in place in a manner that permits this seasonal expansion and contraction.

For example, in our kitchen there is an oak trestle table almost 33" wide. I built it six or eight years ago of solid ⁶⁄₄ white oak joined with cross-grain splines. At either end of the table there is a breadboard end fastened in place with a ploughed

It's important that the rung, slat, arm, and rocker stock be properly seasoned. Bill begins the seasoning process by establishing a solid base for his drying piles.

Then, separating each layer of green lumber with 1" x 1" stickers running perpendicular to the drying material, he builds stacks that sometimes reach 12 feet.

After 3 to 6 months outdoors, the lumber is brought into a heated garage and stickered once again, this time for 4 to 8 weeks, depending on the outside temperature and relative humidity. Notice the fan that keeps the air moving through the stacks.

groove in one edge that is fit over a tongue milled onto the ends of the tabletop's boards. Because I knew the top would expand and contract across its width, I installed the breadboard ends with a single screw coming up through the breadboard end into the tongue on the top's center board. The remainder of the breadboard end is unfastened, simply floating on the tongue. In July, the width of the tabletop aligns nicely with the length of the breadboard end; however, in January, the tabletop has shrunk almost a ¼" across its width, allowing the breadboard ends to protrude beyond the width of the table.

When a woodworker visits a lumberyard that sells cabinet-grade hardwood, that woodworker is assured that the lumber in the yard has been kiln-dried to 6 or 7 or 8 percent. Although the yard workers may never state it plainly, there is behind this assurance the implication that the process of kiln-drying guarantees that the material on sale will always remain at the cited MC, thus guaranteeing the dimensional stability of anything constructed of that material.

Unfortunately, this is not true. All wood, no matter how carefully it is dried, will expand and contract in response to seasonal fluctuations in relative humidity and temperature. This is certainly true of air-dried stock. But it is also true of kiln-dried stock because a board (which is really nothing more than a bundle of tiny tubes that are designed to conduct water) will always seek a state of equilibrium with the moisture content of the surrounding atmosphere unless its every surface is completely sealed against that atmosphere.

For the chair-maker, the problem of moisture management is not so much a design consideration as it is process consideration. With the exception of those chairs having wide board seats fastened to a mortise-and-tenon frame, no allowance for expansion and contraction of wide panels is necessary.

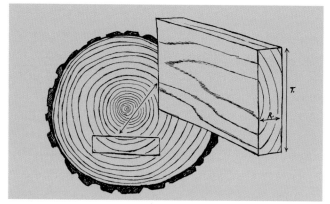

This board will shrink twice as much in a tangential direction (T) as it will in a radial direction (R). Lengthwise shrinkage will be negligible.

However, the chair-maker can make use of the shrinkage of drying wood to create powerful mortise-and-tenon joinery.

GREEN-WOOD JOINERY

If a dry rung tenon is placed into a mortise that has been cut into a wet post, the post and its mortise will shrink onto that rung tenon, locking it permanently in place.

Green-wood joiners don't all apply this principle in the same manner. Makers of country chairs tend to work their wood very green. However, makers of Shaker reproductions and makers of other, more formal post-and-rung chairs tend to work their wood a little drier—for several very good reasons.

First, although fresh-cut wood is much easier to cut and shape with shaving and with turning tools than is dry wood, fresh-cut stock introduces significant amounts of moistureto the chair-making operation which induces rust. A second reason for not turning fresh-cut wood is that it can't be sanded. Although in a perfect world skew planing would produce a mirror-smooth surface on every part, I always find, in my shop, that some sanding is required.

Third, the chair-maker must realize that shrinkage is not consistent in all directions. Turned forms are likely to shrink almost twice as much tangentially as they are radially. (*See drawing opposite.*) This means that a form turned from fresh-cut wood to a perfectly round cross section will not be round after it has dried. It will, in fact, have taken on the pronounced cross section of an oval.

And last, if a chair is assembled with posts that are too wet, *too much* mortise shrinkage can occur, splitting the posts. Granted, an experienced hand with green wood can make relatively accurate estimates of a post's capacity for shrinkage by feel, but the problem of split posts can be completely eliminated by allowing the post stock to dry to the 20 percent range before turning.

Many makers of post-and-rung chairs look for a moisture content neither too wet nor too dry. I work with post stock in the 20 percent moisture range. Newly sawn surfaces will feel slightly damp but not wet. Into these posts I fit rung tenons that have been oven-dried to 2 percent or less. This, together with liberal gluing, produces joints that stay together but don't introduce the complications of fresh-cut wood.

Makers of traditional chairs (John Alexander is one example) are meticulous about the relative grain orientation of posts and rungs. Additionally, these makers of traditional chairs also often flatten the vertical faces of each tenon. The reason for these procedures is to make post splitting less likely as the post stock dries after chair assembly. I choose to align the grain so that it is most visually appealing.

SEATING MATERIAL

Historically, country chairs were seated with thin strips of the hickory tree's inner bark or with ash splint, which is obtained by pounding wet ash logs so that the grain separates and can then be peeled away in strips of loosened wood. Both are excellent seating materials, but both are expensive to buy and difficult to harvest on your own.

When seating a chair of this type, I use a substitute, rattan splint, which is taken from the same plant that produces caning material. This product—which is similar in appearance to ash splint—is widely available in consistently high quality at reasonable prices from mail order suppliers.

Shaker tape, the seating material of choice for most Shaker reproductions, is a dyed, nonelastic cotton tape that is woven over the seat rungs, typically over a cushion and in a checkerboard pattern. (Refer to Chapter Eight, on weaving seats, for details of both splint and tape and how to use them.) Like rattan splint, it's widely available from mail order sources in a consistently high quality. However, price varies widely. To get fully discounted prices even from the suppliers of professionals, it's necessary, of course, to order a considerable quantity of tape.

21

ADHESIVES

For several years, my shop was devoted to furniture repair and refinishing. During that time, I worked on hundreds of chairs. A few were very old and needed a complete regluing, since the hide glue with which they'd been assembled had become dry and brittle. But most of the chairs that came in my door arrived with a single broken part and a full complement of intact glue joints.

The older chairs, those in which the glue had largely failed, were easy to repair. Most of the joints could be disassembled using nothing more than my hands. As a result, I could, with confidence, give the customer a price on the day they delivered their chairs to my shop.

But the newer chairs, those typically arriving with a single broken part, were another matter. It was easy to make the replacement part, but installing it meant that the chair would have to be partially or, in some cases, fully disassembled. Before repairing these newer chairs, I always explained to the customer that the bill could be determined only after I had completed the repair because I couldn't predict what kind of trouble I would have disassembling the intact glue joints.

The problem is that the glues available to the woodworker are just *too good*. In terms of strength, any of the three major types of woodworking glues are more than satisfactory.

Hide glue is often cited as the best choice for furniture repair and assembly because a piece that has been put together with hide glue can be easily disassembled when repairs are needed. I would agree that this is true if, at the time of disassembly, the hide glue is old and brittle; but my experience suggests that joints assembled with this adhesive when they are fresh are still very difficult to break. True, water will dissolve the glue, but sometimes it is almost impossible to get that water into the joint.

The only other seating material used on the chairs appearing in this book is rush. The finest rush is made from dried cattail leaves twisted into a sturdy cord by the chair bottomer at the time of seat weaving. This is a fairly arcane discipline, about which I know very little. The four chairs in this book that have rush seats left my shop unseated and were taken then by the customer to someone specializing in weaving this type of seating material. In recent years, substitute products, which offer a similar look and easier handling, have made their appearance.

I've used hot, wet towels wrapped around the joint, hypodermic injections of hot water directly into the joint, and I have even drilled tiny holes into the joint and filled them with hot water. And still sometimes, disassembly comes down to brute force.

The one real advantage of hide glue—its relatively long open time (open time refers to the period after glue application that a joint can be safely shifted in order to bring parts into the proper alignment)—rarely comes into play in the chair-maker's shop. When I assemble a chair, I first assemble the front ladder, a process taking no more than five minutes, often less. I then assemble the back ladder. This may take a little longer, but rarely more than six or seven minutes, a time span still comfortably within the open-time limits for both yellow and white glues. I then bring these two ladders together in a third gluing session, one in which the side rungs are set into place. But even here, the assembly time is still within the limits established for both yellow and white glues.

I opt for convenience and choose the adhesives that combine enormous strength with ease of application and a long shelf life. On my bench there is a bottle of white glue and one of yellow glue; I choose the one that is closest to my hand.

ABRASIVES

In December of 1995, just after Christmas, I visited Windsor chair-maker David Wright in Kentucky, in order to do a profile of his work for "Woodwork" magazine. During my visit, David turned a baluster chair leg from cherry, which he gave to me. It now sits on my desk, serving there as both an inspiration and an accusation.

Having watched the entire turning process, I know that no abrasives were used in the creation of that baluster leg. However, the surface is smooth and clean. It is already prepared for the first coat of finish. I envy David's skill.

More often than not, I rely on abrasives to clean up roughened areas before finishing. If, like me, you struggle to get that perfectly smooth skew-planed surface, let me suggest high-quality shop rolls from a supplier such as The Sanding Catalogue. These cloth-backed rolls are tough enough for use on the lathe and the abrasives are very sharp, cutting rapidly, speeding this process.

Chapter Three
HAND TOOLS

The hand tools in my shop can be divided into two categories.

The first category is comprised of those tools used to perform the various maintenance operations that are an inevitable part of any shop's operation. This group includes the wrenches used to change saw blades, the screwdrivers used to mount stock on a turning faceplate, the Allen wrenches used to lock a drill press table into the required angles. Strictly speaking, these are not woodworking tools, but nevertheless no woodworking shop can function without them, and any shop will, in the course of time, naturally accumulate a number of these tools.

The second category includes all those tools with which I actually mark, cut, and shape chair parts. These are the tools that make woodworking fun.

MEASURING AND MARKING

Perhaps the most important tools in this second category are those used to measure and mark, and perhaps the most important of these is my six-foot folding carpenter's rule, which I put to constant use—as an aid in selecting material appropriate for a particular chair, as a guide when setting the table-saw fence prior to ripping out turning stock, at the lathe to estimate diameters, and at the planer to determine the thicknesses of slats, rockers, and arms.

Although many turners keep a rack of calipers hanging above their lathes, each pair set to one of the critical diameters for a turned part, I use only a single pair that are set to the diameter of the rung tenons. Other diameters are measured by eye and confirmed with my folding rule. Most precise measurement, however, is done by transferring information from my layout sticks directly to the chair parts, a process that will be discussed in some detail a bit later on.

Once the measurements have been transferred to the wood from the rule or the layout sticks, the locations must be marked, and to do this I use several types of marking instruments. When preparing to chunk up rough lumber to the approximate length, I use a carpenter's pencil with a thick lead because its marks are easily seen on rough lumber. When, with my line-marking gauge (the use of which is explained in Chapter Six, on mortising), I'm making the lines along the length of a post on which I will later locate the centers of the various mortises, I use a fine-pointed No. 2 lead pencil because its lines are easily removed.

But when I'm marking the centers of mortises along those lines on back posts that will later be bent, I use an ink pen, because the process of steaming the posts prior to bending can sometimes obliterate pencil lines.

When marking the sides of the slat mortises on the back posts, I use a small wooden-handled knife since its cut line provides my chisels with secure and accurate placement for paring the mortises to their final size.

The awl and the compass are the last of the marking tools that see any use in my shop. The awl is used to provide a location for the center points of the lathe's drive and tail center, while the compass is used to mark out the stock that will later be band-sawn and turned to form the mushroom caps used on certain Shaker chair reproductions.

One of the more intimidating aspects of chair-making is the need for angles that measure something other than 90 degrees. Unfortunately for those craftsmen trained in the creation of parts from straight and square stock, chair-making does require the accurate establishment of non-right angles. These angles can be achieved on the lathe or on the drill press through the use of the mortise jig and the tilting table. But sometimes it's necessary to take a reading of the angles off a particular chair.

For example, I'm often asked to duplicate a client's chair, and in order to do that I have to identify its angles. It isn't necessary to translate that angle into a number. It is necessary, however, to transfer that angle to either my jig or to the drill press itself. I do have a commercially made bevel square that is designed for this type of application, but its legs are too short to yield meaningful readings on chair parts since chair parts—rungs and posts—are often tapered. Laying a conventional short-legged bevel square against a tapered rung produces flawed readings because those short legs simply follow the tapers. To overcome this, I made a bevel square out of wood, equipping it with legs long enough (about 12 inches) to read the angle—not the taper—on chair parts.

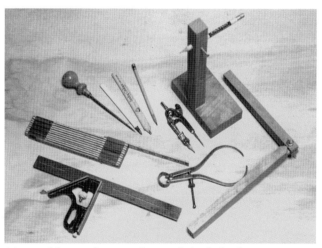

My marking and measuring tools include the try square, my six-foot folding carpenter's rule, an awl, an ink pen, a thick-leaded carpenter's pencil, a fine-point No. 2 lead pencil, a compass, and a pair of calipers.

Two shop-made measuring and marking tools are among the most important in my shop:

The wooden bevel square on the right allows me to transfer chair angles from samples to the drill press or to the drill press jigs described in Chapter Six.

In the upper left is the marking gauge, which, when placed on my lathe table, allows me to run straight lines along the length of lathe-mounted stock.

A framing square is essential during the assembly process. My post-and-rung chairs (this includes two-thirds of the chairs in this book) are assembled in sections. I first assemble the front ladder, which consists of both front posts and the rungs connecting those posts. These rungs and posts must come together with their centerlines at 90-degree angles. The joinery—round mortises cut on the drill press housing tenons formed on the lathe—will establish these angles, but it is possible to get things a little skewed when squeezing the tenons into their mortises with pipe clamps.

To check the angles, I stand the freshly assembled front ladder (with the glue still wet) on my bench and lean a framing square against it with one leg of the square on the bench top. Then, by aligning the square's second (upright) leg with either post, I read the angle. If it's not 90 degrees—the angle at which the two legs of the framing square meet—I rack the ladder until it comes into the proper alignment. To do this, I put on the bench top the foot of the post marking the corner of the front ladder with the most acute angle and press down on the top of the other post, directing the force through the ladder down to the foot resting on the bench top. This racking action will correct the ladder's angles. I then lay the ladder on my bench to check for twist, making corrections by twisting the ladder in my hands until it comes into alignment.

Back ladders, consisting of the back posts and any slats and/or rungs that connect them, are a bit more tricky. Typically, the back ladder spreads as it rises from the floor, so that the top slat is an inch or more wider shoulder to shoulder than is the bottom rung. This means that, when standing upright with the correct angles, neither of the back posts will be 90 degrees from the bench top. A framing square, however, can still be used to evaluate the alignment of the back ladder. I do this by standing the ladder upright on my bench top, holding the upright leg of the square so that, at its intersection with the bottom leg, the square is just touching the inside face of one of the back posts. I raise my eye to the top of the upright leg of the square. Then, with my eye, I measure the distance between the top of the square's upright leg and the inside face of the post. Typically, this will be in the range of ¼ to ⅜ of an inch. I then evaluate the other back post in the same way. Any disagreement in these estimated measurements is corrected by racking the ladder.

To check the back ladder for twist, I stand it on the floor and sight down on it from above. Any visible error is corrected by twisting the frame in my hands while I lock the feet of the posts against my shoes.

The try square is used to lay out slat lengths and tenons prior to assembly.

Wooden vise jaws not only protect the work being clamped, but they also extend and widen the vise's gripping surfaces. The small black lever to the right of the vise screw just below the handle is the quick-release lever. This allows the vise jaws to be swiftly moved from one setting to the next without any protracted and tiresome turning of the screw.

CLAMPING

No useful woodwork can be done without clamping tools.

Although their primary function in the practice of casework—holding parts together while glue dries—doesn't apply to the kind of chair-making on which this book is focused, clamping tools are, nevertheless, essential in the execution of a dozen different chair-making operations.

The most important clamping tool for the maker of post-and-rung chairs is the bench vise. (For the maker of Windsor chairs, the most important clamping tool is probably the shaving horse.) For years I used a twenty-five-dollar Sears vise, which has recently been replaced by a much better vise with a quick-release lever. However, if the threaded fitting in which the screw turned hadn't crumbled on my Sears model, I never would have replaced it, because it never failed to perform.

I use the vise to hold turning stock while it's being centered. I also use it to hold chair slats, arms, and rockers while their band-sawn edges are given a final shaping and sanding. And inevitably, in the course of any workday, other situations will arise in which the bench vise is essential. A machine-shop bench vise in my shop gets little use, although some chair-makers do use this tool to hold stock while it is being worked with a drawknife. It's particularly suited for this operation since its height above the bench top allows room for movement of the drawknife's handles.

In my shop when I use the drawknife (primarily in the shaping of certain types of chair arms), I install a set of wooden puppets on a pipe clamp, then tighten the middle of the pipe clamp in my

Although not a complete inventory of my clamping devices, this photo shows those most used in the chair-making process.

Notice the bar clamp shown in the upper left: When the pipe running between the two wooden puppets is clamped into a vise, a chair arm blank can be held so it can be worked with shaving tools.

Notice also the ¾" hole drilled on the inside of the puppet facing the viewer. The ⅝" tenon on one end of the arm is placed in this hole, while the other end is trapped in a hollow dished into the inside face of the other puppet.

vise. The puppets raise the work high enough above the height of the bench top to permit me to work it with a drawknife.

The jig in which I hold chair posts for the drilling of front and back mortises on the drill press must be able to be placed in a number of locations on the drill press table. To hold it in place once I've positioned it, I use a pair of short pistol-grip bar clamps with triggers which allow me to pump up the clamping pressure. I find them quick and easy in this application. I also use these clamps when I'm holding a back post in place on the bench top while chopping out a set of slat mortises.

I use pipe clamps when assembling the various sections of a chair. They allow me to push oversized tenons into their mortises without breaking the chair parts. To do this, I apply glue to each surface of each joint, then tap the tenons into place with a soft mallet, after which I seat the tenons deeply in their mortises by carefully applying pressure with the pipe clamps.

Although I'm inclined in most cases to recommend cheap tools, my experience suggests that good pipe clamps are worth the money. I have eight or ten of the cheaper variety that I never use because the tail stop is locked in place with a cam that must be tapped by a hammer—an inconvenience—and also because the screw fittings often don't work smoothly. These problems can complicate the process of assembly, a process that must take place quickly and without any significant hitches—or the chair can be lost.

In the shop, when I reach for a pipe clamp, I always choose Pony clamps with the multiple-disk clutch on the tail stop. This clutch locks the stop in place without tapping and is easily moved to new positions along the pipe. Also, there is never a problem with the screw fittings on my Pony clamps. Their smooth functioning helps to make the process of assembly move painlessly along.

In addition to the clamps already mentioned, I make use of a number of miscellaneous clamps in a number of miscellaneous situations. For example, my wooden lathe toolrests are held in place with pairs of C-clamps. I use spring clamps of various sizes when gluing mushroom-cap turning stock onto the scrap to which my lathe faceplate is screwed, and I also use several tiny C-clamps to hold the otherwise inadequate fence on my jointer in position.

TAPPING AND HAMMERING

The traditional carpenter's hammer, in its various sizes and weights, is not likely to see much use in the chair-making shop. I have both a 16 oz. and 13 oz., neither of which leaves the tool chest unless I'm doing some kind of building repair—with one exception: When I'm tapping a wedge into place in its notch in the end grain of a chair post, I do use the 16 oz. carpenter's hammer. The ping of the metal hammer head changes pitch as I strike a fully seated wedge, signaling me to go on to the next wedge.

As you can see from the tattered duct tape surrounding the head of the mallet at the top of the photo, I'm not much concerned with the physical appearance of my tools. I am, instead, concerned with their ability to do the work they need to do.

I do, however, make frequent use of two soft-headed mallets. One, a 22 oz. deadblow mallet for which I paid far too much money, is used when fixing turning stock onto the spurs of the lathe's drive center. A couple of raps with this mallet on the tail end of the turning stock presses those spurs deeply into the end grain. Too many blows, however, can split the stock, but I think that has happened to me only once.

My most important mallet is one that I pulled out of the bargain bin at a local lumberyard. It cost a dollar. This bargain-bin mallet is short-handled, with a soft rubber head weighing less than 8 oz., and I can't, therefore, generate any power when I swing it. This means it can be used freely when dry-fitting a complicated back ladder. I can also use it freely when disassembling a chair someone has brought into the shop for regluing. Its virtue is in its light weight, its extremely short handle, and its very soft head—all of which make it unlikely that anything struck with this mallet will be broken. However, in order to hold the crumbling head together, I've frequently had to wrap it with duct tape.

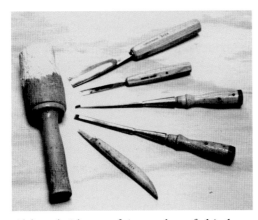

Although I have a fair number of chisels and gouges, I always reach for the few shown here, which can be persuaded to do an astonishing variety of work. The wooden mallet, turned for me by my dad from a limb of hard maple, has seen considerable use in the shop.

MORTISING AND CARVING

Except for the benches, every slat mortise on every chair pictured in this book was chopped out by hand. I could cut the mortises on the drill press with a mortising attachment. Or I could buy any of several reasonably priced mortising machines. Or for just a bit more, I could buy an overarm router, the tool with which Charles Harvey, a contemporary maker of first-rate Shaker reproduction chairs, cuts his mortises.

But I don't like to spend money on new machinery, and power tools are noisy and dirty. Besides, I like the process of cutting mortises by hand. It requires a certain amount of skill, and our technology-driven lives permit us too few chances to acquire and demonstrate manual skills.

So, aside from occasionally using the drill press, for the most part I have continued to chop them out by hand using a ¼" mortise chisel (ground ¹⁄₃₂" narrower to permit me to more easily cut a mortise that is exactly ¼" in width), a ½" paring chisel (I use this tool to shave the mortise sidewalls), and a maple mallet my dad turned and gave me for Christmas several years ago. With these simple, silent, and inexpensive hand tools, the slat mortises for a four-slat chair can be cut in an hour and a half.

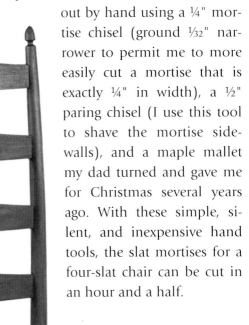

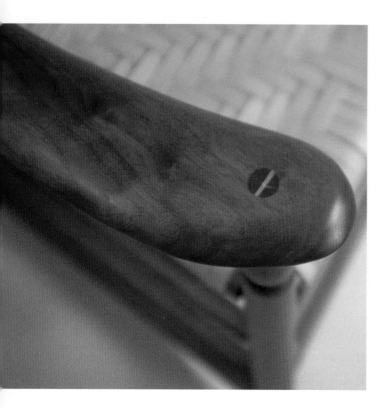

Aside from two incised curlicues on the top slat of one of the rockers, the only situation in this book requiring carving tools is the formation of certain types of chair arms. To shape them, I use two carving gouges and the paring chisel mentioned above. One of the gouges, a 25mm No. 5, is used to rough-in the crowned bevels on the end grain of the chair arm. The other gouge, an 8mm No. 5, is used to clean up the depressions left by the larger tool. The paring chisel is used to pare the end grain to its final shape.

One last tool that should be mentioned in this category is a wooden-handled knife with a straight blade. The blades is about 1½" long. A knife like this is available from a number of different suppliers under several different names. In my shop, this knife is an all-purpose tool that sees duty as a marking knife, an aid in creating sharp carved lines, and a scraper to remove pencil lines from chair posts prior to sanding.

SHAVING

Some tools, like the drawknife and the spokeshave, are just fun to use. Why?

First, I think it's because they do what they are designed to do in such an efficient manner. Both tools rapidly remove waste, leaving behind surfaces that, although flattened into planes by their straight cutting edges, have a glossy, sheared appearance, surfaces offering a satisfying smoothness to the touch. Second, they are both clean tools. Their passage leaves behind thick shavings instead of shreds of airborne dust. But perhaps most important is the way these tools feel in the woodworker's hands. Unlike anything driven by an electric motor—characterized by noise and vibration—they intimately engage the craftsman with the work. These hand tools allow him to feel in his wrists, arms, and hands the contours being shaped.

The drawknife consists of a thick steel blade with a handle at either end. Over the years, this tool has been made in dozens of different configurations, each designed for specific woodworking applications. Windsor chair-makers, for example, use a drawknife with a bent blade, referred to as an inshave, to clean up adze marks left in the dished areas of chair seats. Coopers use drawknives in many different shapes, among them the scorp, which is a drawknife in which the blade forms a complete circle and is drawn through the wood with a single handle. Sawyers use a straight, oversized (often more than two feet in length) drawknife to remove bark from logs before sawing them—an operation that protects the saw blade from being dulled by the dirt often impacted in the bark. Turners use a shorter, straight drawknife to knock the corners off turning blanks before cutting the blank with lathe tools. In each case, the craftsman chooses a drawknife whose size and shape make it appropriate to the task at hand.

In my shop, I have two drawknives. One, which was used to excavate the seats on a couple of the stools included in this book, is an inshave. The other, which is used nearly every day, is a straight-bladed knife with two handles perpendicular to the blade but canted a few degrees from the plane of the blade in order to make it easier for the craftsman to engage the tool with the work.

I use the second drawknife primarily to shape certain chair arms, but also make frequent use of the tool to round large turning blanks prior to cutting with lathe tools. Sometimes, too, when sorting through my lumber in order to select the material to use for a particular chair, I'll carry the drawknife so that I can shave off the gray, rough-sawn surface material in order to get a better reading of the color and figure of the material beneath.

I like these shaving tools, and find them wondrously versatile when used for the freehand shaping of wood.

Like the drawknife, the spokeshave has a handle at either end. Unlike the drawknife, however, the handles of the spokeshave are in line with, not perpendicular to, that cutting edge, and the spokeshave has a sole that glides across the work that is being shaped. In the case of the modern, metal-bodied spokeshave, the cutting iron protrudes through this sole, much like the iron of a plane. In the case of the classical, wooden-bodied spokeshave the iron actually becomes a part of that sole.

Because of the short, front-to-back length of its sole, the metal-bodied spokeshave offers the woodworker a planing tool that can get into tight places unreachable with a standard plane. The wooden-bodied spokeshave offers this same advantage, plus one other: Its very shallow cutting angle makes it possible to remove very fine shavings even when cutting across end grain.

Although I have a half-round spokeshave, I've rarely used it because the work it is designed to do—cutting rounds—can be done just as easily with a flat-soled spokeshave. My flat-soled shave is used in cleaning up the work of my drawknife or my carving chisels when these tools are used to form chair arms (it is also used to add a radius to the arms of reproduction New Lebanon chairs).

For general shop use, the straight-blade drawknife is the most versatile (and the easiest to sharpen). The flat-soled spokeshave offers the widest range of potential shop applications.

Shaving is a lot like planing. Both require the craftsman to be sensitive to grain direction. Like planing, shaving must be done in the direction pointed at by the rising grain. Often, this means reversing either the workpiece or the tool direction partway along the shaping of the work.

I use the drawknife with the bevel side down, which feels right to me. Other woodworkers use the drawknife with the bevel side up.

Handling the spokeshave requires a bit more feel than does the handling of the drawknife. Anyone picking up a drawknife can make shavings, but the spokeshave requires a little practice.

I set the iron of my spokeshave so that it just peeks through the sole. Then, I begin moving it across the work (it can be pushed or pulled), taking care to keep it in contact with the work at three points: the leading edge, the cutting iron, the heel. According to the shavings produced, I adjust the setting of the iron.

These are the only handsaws that see any use in my chair-making work.

Several of the larger handsaws I have receive little use of any kind. I know this because one of them is still covered with clots of tar from a roofing job I did for a neighbor almost ten years ago. Clearly, if I had actually needed this saw, I would have cleaned the teeth years ago.

PLANING AND SCRAPING

I own a jack plane, as well as a smoothing plane, a block plane, and several molding planes, but the block plane is the only one that sees any action in the chair-making process. This versatile little tool does the final fitting of slats into their mortises.

SAWING

In my shop, there are two backsaws that are frequently used.

One, with 12 tpi (teeth per inch), is used to cut the X's on the end grain of workpieces into which the spurs on the lathe's drive center will be tapped. A workpiece can be centered without the X's, but there is security in knowing that the drive centers on the lathe are positioned solidly into place.

The other backsaw is a small tenon saw with 16 tpi that I use daily in a variety of applications. For example, when shaping the tenon at the rear of the chair arms, I first cut the shoulder with the tenon saw, after which I whittle and rasp the tenon to size. When it is time to put the arm into place, I also use this saw to cut the tenon on the front post to the precise length after I have dry-fitted the arm or the arm and the mushroom cap. But the most important use of this tool is in creating the walls of the notches at the bottom of each post into which rockers are fit.

The block plane shown here on the right is a marvelously capable tool when fitting slats into their mortises. The cabinet scraper, a Stanley 80, is useful in smoothing the surfaces of slats, rockers, and arms after they have been run through the planer, particularly if they are cut from figured wood. The two flexible scrapers shown at the bottom of the photo can be used to smooth surfaces with almost any contour. For example, by bending these in my hands, I was able to remove the tool marks left behind by the inshave in the sculpted areas of the cherry-and-ash stool, the third project in the section of Windsor-style pieces of Chapter Nine, The Projects.

Recently I was given a Stanley No. 80 scraper and, though I haven't had it long, I have found it invaluable in surfacing slats, arms, and rockers cut from figured wood—a job I used to perform with a razor-sharp butt chisel. I also have a pair of flexible steel scrapers that regularly see duty when smoothing hollowed areas like those on the seats of some of the stools presented in the project section of Windsor-style pieces.

POWER TOOLS

Over the past twenty-five years American wood-working has taken two very different courses. As mainstream woodworkers have made their operations more and more equipment-intensive, filling their shops with ever more sophisticated machinery, other woodworkers have turned away from power equipment and have, instead, made shop operations more and more hand-tool-intensive. For some in this second group, the motivation may be a desire to return to the perceived romance of eighteenth-century woodworking, but for others this movement in the direction of hand tool use is more than simple nostalgia; it is, in fact, an admission of the limitations and liabilities inherent in even the most sophisticated power equipment.

Power tools certainly allow work to be done more quickly. With a planer, lumber can be dressed to a consistent thickness as fast as it can be fed into the machine. And power equipment allows a shop owner to hire relatively unskilled workers. After all, anyone can be taught to feed lumber into a planer. But only a skilled craftsman can transform a length of rough 4/4 material into a smoothly finished piece of 3/4 stock using nothing but hand planes, a pair of winding sticks, and a straightedge.

But the power planer is noisy and dirty. When it runs, the shop is a mind-jangling place in which to work. Hand planes are, by contrast, quiet and clean. When they are in use, reflection is possible. In a quiet shop, it is possible to think about what one is doing. And it is this reflection, coupled with the sensitivity possible with the deft manipulation of hand tools, that has encouraged many contemporary woodworkers to turn away from the speed of power equipment and return to the subtleties of the drawknife, the spokeshave, and carving gouges.

Although in principle I prefer to work with hand tools, in actual practice I use both power and hand tools, trying to match each type with the tasks for which, in my opinion, it is best suited.

I use power equipment for the brute work of ripping and planing and resawing, as well as for the drilling of rung mortises, because I find that the drill press performs this critical task more accurately and efficiently than can be done with a brace and bit. However, for other operations—the cutting of slat mortises, the shaping of chair arms, the cutting of rocker notches—I use hand tools.

ESSENTIALS

Although it would be possible to make any of the chairs pictured in this book without power tools (such as the beautiful shaved Shaker-style chair of Owen Rein shown here and in the Gallery section), it is much easier—although less pleasant—to have the assistance of at least three power bench tools: a band saw, a drill press, and a lathe. Additionally, if money permits, I would recommend adding a table saw (useful in a number of situations), a radial arm saw (for chunking up turning stock to the approximately correct length), and a jointer (for straightening turning stock).

None of these need be expensive models. Mine are not, although all needed to be modified or at least augmented with jigs to meet the needs of a chair-maker's shop.

Turning stock must be rendered into pieces of the appropriate cross section. Traditional chair-makers start with a section of log and split it with wedges, a froe, and a club. This method does work, but it is strenu-ous work that also can be wasteful of material. The method of choice for most makers of Shaker-style chairs requires either a band saw or a table saw to rip out turning blanks. Also, material for slats, arms, and rockers must be resawn to the proper thicknesses, then profiled to the proper shapes—jobs for which the band saw is eminently suitable.

The second essential power tool is the drill press. Mortises can be drilled without one, but for makers of Shaker-style chairs the drill press can mean the difference between effortless success and intense frustration in this most critical operation. However, the drill press requires some fairly elaborate accessories to allow the chair-maker to achieve effortless chair mortising. These accessories are a set of particular shop-made jigs—which are discussed in detail in Chapter Six, on mortising.

The most important power tool in the chair-maker's shop is a lathe that will, at a safe speed, spin the work against your tool. Mine is an inexpensive Sears lathe with a tail stock that slides on a two-inch steel tube. Ideally, your lathe should be equipped with an indexing head that enbles the turner to divide accurately the circumference of lathe-turned cylinders. However, there are other ways that this indexing can be accomplished.

Owen Rein

35

POWER TOOL SAFETY

I have formalized a checklist of safety rules based on the practices that I attempt to follow in my shop.

SAFETY CHECKLIST

1. Wear eye protection.

Although twenty years ago, I routinely operated power equipment without eye protection, today the habit is so solidly established that I'm psychologically incapable of turning on a machine unless I've first put on my goggles.

Even some hand tool operations require eye protection. For example, when chopping out slat mortises, I slip on my goggles because the geometry of the mortise sends chips popping up in the general direction of the face each time a blow is struck on the chisel with the mallet.

2. Wear hearing protection.

I didn't start wearing hearing protection until six or eight years ago, and by then it was a little late, as I now have a significant and permanent hearing loss in both ears, exacerbated by the persistent ringing of tinnitus. Now, in an effort to preserve the hearing that is left, I use plugs that fit into the ear canal as well as tightly fit muffs that cover the outer ear.

3. Keep all blades and knives sharp.

As they become dull, the blades on a table saw or a band saw start to wander, making accurate machining difficult—and dangerous. This is particularly true if the operator tries to force the dull blade and the work into the proper alignment.

Hand tools, too, must be kept sharp. Planes, shaves, chisels, gouges, etc., do not work efficiently when dull, and can encourage the woodworker to apply more force than is necessary. This extra force not only increases the likelihood of barked knuckles and chisel and gouge nicks on the craftsman's hands, it can also result in damaged work.

4. Treat the table saw with respect.

This is the only tool in my shop that really frightens me.

A. Use a blade guard with anti-kickback pawls.

B. Use push sticks.

With these, hands can be kept at least a foot from the blade at all times.

C. Never stand directly behind the work being sawn.

The saw can fling a loose rip back toward the operator with amazing force.

D. Never use the table saw for resawing thick stock.

Yes, the tool can perform this operation, and yes, I have used it for this purpose, but I've never seen a way to do it safely. Resawing should always be done on the band saw.

E. With the saw off, rehearse any operations that are tricky or unfamiliar.

Then, if the operation seems unsafe, don't perform it. Instead, look for alternative approaches.

Notes on Safety Rules A through E

These rules apply to the table saw as it is used in my chair-making shop. Other safety measures are necessary when the saw is used to perform different types of work. Consult the owner's manual.

Rule D, like all of these rules, is based on my experience. My father, a cabinetmaker with over forty years of experience, whose work was featured in "Woodwork No. 31," does use the table saw to resaw thick stock. But his method is a unorthodox and I can't fully endorse it.

With the work stood on edge, he makes two passes across the table saw, one cutting into the top edge, the other into the bottom edge. A small hinge of wood is left between the two cuts, so the resawn stock never separates, eliminating the most dangerous part of table-saw resawing: removing the resawn stock from the area of the blade. That small hinge of wood is then sawn through on the band saw.

5. Use blade guards and push blocks when operating the jointer.

Push blocks (I prefer those with foam pads underneath, because the wooden variety can still slide on the work) permit the operator to move stock over the cutting head without risking contact with the knives in the event that the hand slips. And hands do slip.

6. Use caution when operating the drill press and the band saw.

Dad once said that he thought the band saw was the most dangerous tool in his shop. He didn't actually mean that this tool is inherently more dangerous than the table saw.

Instead, he meant that its passive nature can be misleading. Unlike the table saw, which screams and whines as it tears through 6/4 oak and hard maple, the band saw putts along in relative quiet. Likewise, the drill press has an essentially passive nature, going unobtrusively about its business. Nevertheless, both tools are capable of inflicting serious harm on the inattentive operator.

7. Don't operate machinery under the influence of drugs or alcohol or when exhausted. And most important, don't operate machinery when you're angry.

Craftsmen who wouldn't dream of turning on the table saw after drinking a couple of beers will turn on that same saw when they are angry and frustrated—and therefore careless. In the shop, anger can be as debilitating as alcohol.

8. Think.

If an operation seems dangerous, then it probably is.

37

Chapter Five
TURNING

When I began making chairs, we didn't have any money to invest in good tools. I was a schoolteacher in a rural Ohio district, and even though my wife also worked—as a school secretary—with two kids, a mortgage and car payments there was no surplus and little in the way of savings that we would have felt comfortable tapping for the purchase of tools. Therefore, if post-and-rung chairmaking had absolutely required expensive tooling, I would have been unable to attempt it.

At that time, I had a collection of homeowner-type bench tools paid for with money made doing furniture repair and custom casework. There was a table saw, a 4" jointer, a radial-arm saw and a small band saw, plus a pretty good collection of hand tools. What I didn't have was a lathe.

After months of dreaming about creating furniture that people could actually sit in, I went shopping—and every price I saw scared me. $1400? $2200? For a lathe?

Most books on woodworking advise the beginner to buy the best possible tools. And that makes good sense because it's the beginning woodworker who most needs the quality of good tools. But by nature, I'm disinclined to take that approach. I might buy a router, but only when I had a job requiring a router that would pay me enough to cover the cost of the new tool. And the router I chose would not be the best on the market; it would, instead, be the cheapest that I believed could be persuaded to do the necessary work.

Recognizing the shortcomings of my conservatism, I also know that cheap tools can present the woodworker with some intriguing challenges: How can that cheap jointer be augmented so that it will accurately joint long boards? (Maybe a wooden roller on a shop-built extension of the outfeed table.) How can that cheap drill press be modified so that it will accurately drill chair mortises? (Look at the mortising jig pictured in the next chapter.)

38

When I saw the prices of good lathes, I shuddered and turned away. And although I was pretty sure I'd be getting a lot less tool, I did what I'd done in the past when faced with the cost of good machinery: went to Sears. And for $220, plus tax, they sold me a lathe.

The bed was too short. And the only way to change the speed was to shut the power off and move the drive belt from one set of pulleys to another. And the mechanism for advancing the tail center never did work as advertised. But it was a lathe, and I was confident about finding a way to use it to produce chair parts.

As it came from the box, the lathe could be used to turn nothing longer than a table leg, as there was only 36" between centers. Since chair-making often requires 45" or more between centers, some modifications had to be made.

First, I ordered a second mounting foot for the tube on which the tail stock slides. When it arrived, I removed the tube from its position in the head stock assembly and moved the entire tube 12" down the bench, inserting the second mounting foot in the tube's head stock end. This gave me the necessary distance between centers.

(For anyone wishing to modify a Sears lathe in the same way, let me add a cautionary note: Several weeks after lengthening the lathe bed, I was turning a chair's back post, and the turning blank began behaving strangely, lurching away from my gouge. As I reached for the switch, the turning blank—all 46" of it—lifted lazily from the centers, rapped me

on the shoulder, and sailed across the shop. I wasn't hurt but I was surprised. The square nut that is supposed to wedge the body of the mounting foot against the steel tube of the lathe body, holding it firmly in place, had loosened. As a result, the tail stock, which rides on that tube, was rocking back and forth, breaking down the center. A friend then welded the two mounting feet to the tube and eliminated the problem.

A chair post is mounted in my modified lathe.

This incident, however, points out one of the risks of modifying machinery. In its original configuration, with the head stock end of the tube held in place by a fat setscrew, the square nut in the mounting foot was probably enough to hold the tube in place; but as I had modified it, with both ends of the tube held in place by a pair of square nuts wedged against the tube, the strain proved to be too much.)

Two other modifications had to be made. Because the toolrest also slides on the steel tube, moving that tube a foot down the bench meant that I no longer had access to the end of the turning nearest the head stock. To solve this problem and to make the production of chair parts more efficient, I made wooden toolrests the full length of the various chair parts. I simply clamp these to the bench, turn on the lathe, and begin turning. And I made one other change: Because the mechanism for advancing the tail stock center didn't work, I sawed off the lever that locked that center into place, which allowed me to get my long toolrests into a closer proximity to the work being turned.

The entire tail stock is then nudged down the bed, blows from a dead-blow mallet pushing the center into place in the stock's end grain.

What I didn't know at the time is that these early decisions would come to shape nearly every aspect of the chair-making process as it has been practiced in my shop.

If you're lucky enough to have a really good lathe, you could probably skip much of this chapter on turning techniques. But if, like me, you don't have the money that such a tool requires, there may be some ideas here that you can

put into practice in your own shop because, even though I don't do things the same way as many other turners, my methods allow chair parts to be produced quickly and efficiently using my inexpensive Sears lathe.

TURNING PREPARATION

My collection of turning tools is small, consisting of a 1¼" roughing gouge, ¼" and ¾" spindle gouges, 1" and ½" skew chisels, and a 1" butt chisel. (There is also a pair of calipers that I use to check tenon diameter.) When faced with a form that simply can't be coaxed from these tools, I regrind an old parting tool to the right shape.

In order to turn the mushroom caps seen on several of the chairs pictured in this book, a faceplate is also required. Briefly, this is a metal disk with a diameter of about four inches—they're available in other diameters—equipped with a screw fitting designed to turn onto the lathe's drive spindle. Six screw holes perforate the metal disk to permit the screw mounting of turning blanks.

After band-sawing a mushroom-cap turning blank to the approximate diameter, I fix that blank onto a piece of scrap wood using white or yellow glue. I then turn woodscrews into the scrap, passing through the holes in the lathe faceplate. (I put a disk of newspaper into the glue joint between the scrap and the turning stock. This permits breaking the mushroom cap free from the scrap by tapping a chisel point into the glue joint after turning.)

If I'm turning a heavier disk, I'll screw it directly to the faceplate. This does, however, leave screw holes on one side of the turned disk, a circumstance the woodworker must take into consideration when planning the piece.

My spindle turnings begin with four-sided rips. Occasionally, for a very large turning, I'll relieve the corners with a drawknife after centering the stock in the lathe and locking it in place with the index-ing head locking pin; but for stock of a modest cross section—such as that needed for Shaker chair reproductions—I don't take the time to relieve cor-ners prior to turning. I've found that, using my roughing gouge on lathe-mounted stock, the cor-ners of a four-sided turning blank can be knocked off in seconds, much less time than it takes to pro-duce an octagon with a drawknife or a jointer.

If a 1⅜" finished diameter is needed for a post, I rip the stock to a turning blank 1½" on a side. (When turning posts with diameters of more than 1⅜", I begin with similarly oversized turning stock.) Then, before centering the blank in the lathe, I sight along its length for evidence of bow, twist, or crook. If any of these defects is present, I run the stock over the jointer for correction. The goal isn't to create a perfectly smooth, flat surface on my turning stock. Instead, the goal is to create squares or rectangles on each end of the turning blank, the centers of which are also the centers of a 1⅜" cylinder running through the length of each turning blank. Failing to straighten crooked turn-ing stock before centering—particularly in the case of turning blanks for long back posts—almost always means that one side of the post cylinders will end up flat because there is insufficient mater-ial on that one side of the turning blanks. *(See drawing to the right.)*

It is also important at this stage to look for defects in the turning blank. Some—a pea-sized knot, a check, a streak of sapwood—may disquali-fy the piece either structurally or aesthetically for chair use. Other defects are serious enough to make turning dangerous. If, for example, I center a badly cracked turning blank, it can come apart in the lathe. A cracked piece that comes apart while at rest on the workbench is an inconvenience. If, however, that same piece comes apart while spinning at 1350 rpm, my safety is at stake.

Unlike carving tools, which require carefully honed, extremely sharp edges, lathe tools work best when the metal edge is not feathered out quite so finely. This is because these tools take such a beating at the lathe.

While a carving tool might take a half hour to remove a hundred chips of wood, a roughing gouge can remove that much material in a couple of seconds, destroying a carefully constructed edge almost instantly.

I try to move directly from the grinder to the lathe, leaving a small burr on the edge. This burr cuts very quickly and holds up better than a finer edge.

Sometimes, however, when making a finishing cut, I will hone the tool on a Washita stone lubricated with WD-40.

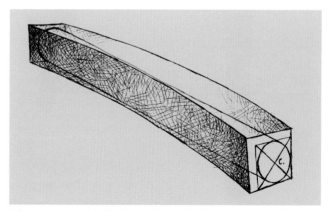

The center (C) of this turning blank is not set at the center of the end-grain face. Instead, it is set at the cen-ter of an imaginary 1⅜" cylinder that runs through the turning blank. (The elements of this drawing are exag-gerated and distorted for clarity.)

After clamping the turning stock into a vise with the end grain up, I use a backsaw to cut a pair of crossing diagonals about ⅛" deep on that end of the turning stock that will be fit onto the drive center. Then, after removing the drive center from the lathe, I tap it into place on the end grain of the turning stock so that the spurs fit snugly into the diagonals and the center point is driven into the exact center of the turning stock.

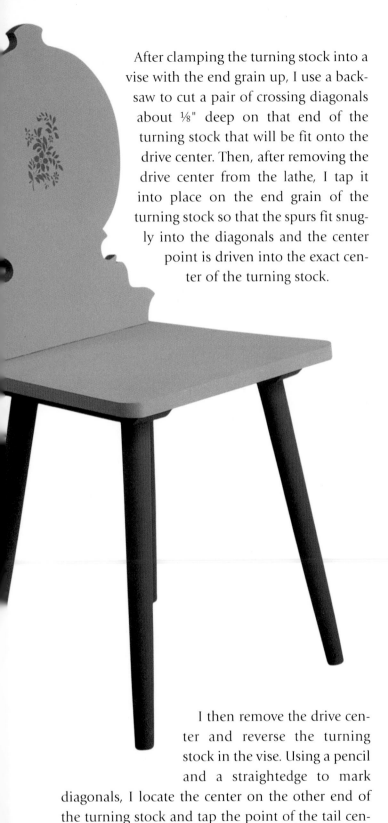

I then remove the drive center and reverse the turning stock in the vise. Using a pencil and a straightedge to mark diagonals, I locate the center on the other end of the turning stock and tap the point of the tail center into the intersection of the diagonals.

Typically, in this way, I will mark the centers on all the parts to be turned for a chair or for a run of chairs. Then, after replacing the drive and the tail centers in their positions on the lathe, I'll mount the turning stock into place on those centers by tapping the tail stock housing with a dead-blow mallet. This ensures that both centers are seated properly. It is particularly important that this be done carefully when mounting the first turning blank in a series, because the two lathe centers also need to be set into their tapered housings after reinsertion.

The heights of my homemade toolrests are not adjustable, and the hickory from which these toolrests were made has worn down, resulting in some low areas, in addition to a slight across-the-board reduction in rest height. Technical manuals stress the importance of establishing just the right rest height for various lathe operations. I've learned to accommodate the low areas and the inadjustable heights for two reasons. First, I didn't know any better. When I began making chair parts, I thought that all lathe operations were performed with a single rest height, so that's what I learned to do. And second, nearly all the turnings produced in my shop have simple silhouettes. Except for mushroom caps on Shaker reproductions, I do no faceplate turning, and the most common shape I form between centers is a gradual taper.

ROUGHING-IN

After clamping my toolrest in place, I take out the 1¼" roughing gouge and begin turning.

Berea, Kentucky, chair-maker Charles Harvey has an enormous Oliver lathe with a rheostat as speed control. This means that with the twist of a wrist, he can adjust the speed of his lathe while it is spinning. He can, therefore, rough-in at one speed, then shift to a higher speed for finishing and sanding.

This is the grip that I use when I'm roughing-in a cylinder (and sometimes when I'm forming shapes with spindle gouges).

Although the photo doesn't show this, the fingers have been cut from the glove to prevent them from being drawn up into the gap between the toolrest and the work.

The work is supported by the fleshy pad at the base of my fingers that is pressed against the back side of the cylinder, while the thumb pressing against the roughing gouge stabilizes the hand and, by extension, the work.

Notice the masking tape wrapped around the glove's palm. This is periodically renewed with fresh tape as the friction with the rough turning wears through to my hand.

After the rung stock has been roughed-in, I use the knife edge of the skew to transfer the tenon locations from the wooden toolrest—on which they've been marked—to the rung stock.

My inexpensive Sears model didn't come well equipped. The only way to adjust the speed of my lathe is to stop the machine, open the cover on the head stock end, and shift the V-belt to another set of pulleys. This is not only inconvenient; it is also time-consuming. What I've learned to do instead is to turn all chair parts at the same speed (1350 rpm), a practice I find safe as long as the turning stock is sound, without structural defects, and as long as the stock is securely mounted in the lathe. Nevertheless, when turning a piece significantly larger than the posts on a Shaker chair—for example, those on a Brewster or Carver chair—I start out at the slowest speed (875 rpm), then move up to a higher speed after the cylinder has been roughed-in.

Although I now turn almost everything at 1350 rpm, when I began turning chair parts, I roughed-in at 875 rpm, then increased the speed for final shaping, increasing it once again for sanding. And I would recommend that turners who haven't yet grown comfortable with the turning of the long, thin spindles that post-and-rung chair-making requires do as I did and rough-in those parts at the slowest possible speed. The only exception to this would be for the back posts—which are discussed below.

There's nothing tricky about roughing-in a rung or a front post. I center the stock, turn on the lathe, and bring the tip of my roughing gouge into the spinning work. Until the corners have been knocked off, I move cautiously, taking light passes. Then as the stock begins to approach a cylindrical shape, I become more aggressive, working the gouge back and forth along the length of the stock, engaging the tool solidly enough to send up a generous arc of chips.

But back posts are another matter. The first back post I ever turned took almost two hours because, although I'd previously done some turning, I'd never worked on anything so long and thin. What I found was that if the gouge were pressed into the work firmly enough to remove material, the post—flexible because of its length—bowed away from the gouge. This bowing resulted in a deep and ugly cut that spiraled around the post.

There seemed to be no middle ground. If I pressed against the turning stock so lightly that it didn't flex, I removed no material. However, if the pressure was hard enough to remove material, the work flexed and the gouge cut a spiral. As a result, those first few back posts were shaped entirely

without skill, relying instead on persistence as I wore away material about as swiftly as water wears away rock. Although this process did eventually produce chair posts, it was clear that if I didn't solve this problem, I wouldn't make any money as a chair-maker. A more efficient way had to be found to turn these long, thin spindles.

I considered a steady rest, but although I now use one for the turning of certain finials, I did not want to inhibit the freedom I'd found in turning the whole length of a piece with the aid of full-length wooden toolrests. Too, moving a steady rest back and forth along the length of the back post turning stock could make the process very time-consuming. What was needed was a quick method, something that would give me the chance to make a little money with these chairs.

Eventually, over a period of months, I found that in order to turn back posts efficiently, two things had to be done.

First, I began using a gloved off-hand as a steady rest. A bare hand provided the support I needed, but the friction generated too much heat.

(I know that some woodworkers see this gloved-hand steady rest as a dangerous practice. If the hand is kept away from the head stock and the fingers are allowed to dangle, keeping only the palm of the hand against the work, there is nothing inherently hazardous about the practice. As a precaution, I do cut the fingers from my turning gloves so that they can't be drawn into the gap between the turning stock and the toolrest. I feel much safer using a gloved hand as a steady rest on the lathe than I do when performing any operation on the table saw.)

After becoming comfortable with this method of turning back posts, I began using it on shorter turning stock as well, because by bringing the thumb of my off-hand down over the top of the work and pressing it against the gouge, I found that I could work safely with complete control at a more aggressive pace, a principle that applied to this shorter stock as well.

The second important change for turning back posts was increasing lathe rpm. It was something I tried, in desperation, when I was unable to think of anything else. Remarkably, what I found was this: At slow speeds, the post stock easily gives ground as the tool is pressed against it. At higher speeds (1350 rpm or greater), the work becomes more resistant to such flexing. I suspect this is because at higher rpm the tool is in more nearly constant contact with the entire circumference of the turning spindle, but I'm not scientist enough to know for sure. But, on a practical level, increasing lathe rpm inhibits the tendency of long spindles to flex away from the lathe tool.

After a couple of passes with a spindle gouge, I check the rung tenon's least diameter with a pair of calipers.

With a 1" butt chisel laid bevel side down on the rest, I scrape away the rest of the tenon waste.

With my skew, a 1/16" bevel is created at the end of the tenon. This bevel prevents the leading edge of the tenon from being caught against the wall of its mortise during assembly.

FORMING RUNG TENONS

After roughing the rung stock to a cylindrical shape, I form the tenons at each end.

The union of rung tenons and post mortises is the most critical element in the chair-making process. Failure to properly control this process inevitably results in a chair that won't stand up under the strain of a person's shifting weight. Over time, glue joints loosen and the chair develops disconcerting creaks. Proper control of this process will, just as inevitably, result in a chair able to provide generations of service to the owner's family.

To a great extent, the success of that union requires efficient management of the moisture content of the wood. As discussed in Chapter Two on materials, dry rung tenons should be fit into mortises cut into wetter posts. Then, as these parts approach a state of moisture equilibrium, the posts shrink and the rungs expand, creating a tight joint.

Additionally, however, this union requires careful work at the lathe in shaping the rung tenons.

I begin the process by transferring tenon locations from the surface of my wooden toolrest to the spinning lathe stock using the knife point of my skew to mark the tenon shoulders. Then, with a ¾" spindle gouge, I rough-in the tenon, checking it several times with a set of calipers.

When the thinnest portion of the tenon has reached the required diameter (⅝" on nearly every chair in this book), I switch to a sharp 1" butt chisel. This is placed bevel side down on the toolrest. The edge is then brought into contact with the work. The chisel acts as a scraper, quickly shaving the entire length of the tenon down to the diameter of its thinnest portion. At this point, I use the calipers to check the diameter of the length of the tenon to make sure that it is consistent from end to end. Any necessary adjustments are made with the butt chisel.

Then, using the skew point, I cut a ¹⁄₁₆" bevel on the end of the tenon opposite the shoulder. This bevel will prevent the end of the tenon from sticking in the mortise as the tenon is being seated under the pressure of a pipe clamp at assembly.

Ideally, these tenons should be cut a few hundredths of an inch oversize. This permits an even tighter joint. However, I've found that the process is relatively forgiving. If the tenon is simply snug at assembly, the glue and the shrinkage will create a strong joint. The only part of this process that is tricky is reading the calipers.

Using calipers require a bit of experience because it is possible to force them over a tenon that is considerably oversized. Even today, after checking thousands of tenons with my calipers, I make a couple of test fittings of a tenon into a mortise cut in a block of scrap before turning a batch of rungs. This gives me an opportunity to check, once again, the feel of the calipers on a tenon that is, in fact, a few hundredths oversize.

SKEW PLANING

With the roughing gouge, I bring the cylinder to within ¹⁄₁₆" of its final maximum diameter. Then, with the skew and ¾" spindle gouge, I begin to form the various required shapes. On the rungs, the tapers are established that lead downhill toward the tenons. On the front posts, I establish the taper at the foot and rough-in whatever shapes are needed below the arms, leaving the work ¹⁄₁₆" over the finished diameter. The only shapes that aren't formed at this time are the finials atop each of the back posts. These are shaped later, after the posts have been marked for the drilling of rung mortises.

Unlike most turners, I don't establish the diameters of the various parts with a parting tool prior to shaping. Instead I just begin shaping those parts with my ¾" spindle gouge and skew, reading the diameters in process—first with my eye, then verifying these estimates with the end of a rule laid across the turning stock. Precision is less important than balancing the various shapes of a chair part against one another.

At this point, I skew-plane. For a year or more, I struggled to learn this technique, and for a year or more periodically dug chunks from turnings when I lost control of the skew and it lurched into the

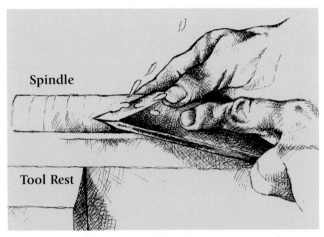

This drawing shows my left-handed approach to skew planing. Right-handers will likely prefer a different grip.

When planing, I try to do two things: First, I lay the bevel of the skew flat atop the spinning work. (It's important that the skew iron remain in contact with the toolrest.) Second, I maintain contact between the cutting edge and the work below the center of the skew's sharpened edge.

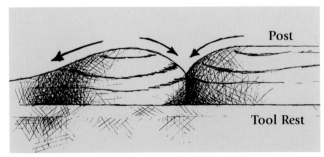

Skew planing should be accomplished downhill as shown in this drawing. Trying to plane uphill against the grain will result in tear-out.

work. At one point, I decided my ½" skew was too narrow. I bought a 1" skew and tried to keep the middle of the skew's edge in contact with the work. But the results were little better. I thought then that my grip was incorrect, so I experimented with different hand postures. The results were the same. Then, while doing a story for "Woodwork" magazine about Charles Harvey, I noticed that he held his skew *upside down* when he planed. When I got home, I tried that too, but the results were no better.

Finally, more as result of determination than skill, I found that, if I was really careful, rungs could be skew-planed by laying the ground bevel of my skew flat on the surface of the turning so that the edge met the work at a very shallow angle. Then, one day, I learned something else about skew-planing. I was preparing the turnings for a curly maple rocker. As usual, I was struggling with the skew. At one point, I stopped turning and simply took a moment to look at what I was doing. With the lathe off, I rehearsed my technique, trying to decide exactly what it was that happened when I lost control. Laying the edge of the tool on the post, and keeping the point of contact near the middle of the skew's width, I rocked the skew back and forth.

I noticed then that the point of the skew—that part of the edge closest to the toolrest—was supported by the rest. I noticed, too, that the other side of the edge—that part farthest from the toolrest—was unsupported. I rocked the skew back and forth and thought about support: The skew had been digging into the work because as I moved the point of contact even slightly above the middle of the skew's wide cutting edge—away from that part of the edge that is supported by the toolrest—the edge was catching on the spinning circumference of the work.

My figured then that a second principle of skew planing was this: In order to avoid these digs, I had to plane only with the lower half of the skew's edge. There, the cutting edge would be supported by the toolrest, and it would be all but impossible for the skew to be twisted in my hand, throwing the edge into the work. *(Refer to the drawings opposite.)*

I switched the lathe on. Then I put the skew against the work at that point on the skew's edge that was closest to the toolrest and began planing.

Suddenly, remarkably, I found that I could plane the long, thin back posts that had once confounded me. I could also plane the vases on the front posts and the disks and balls at the top of the back posts.

To put my thinking to the test, I moved the point of contact between the cutting edge and the spinning work higher than the middle of the skew's edge. Sure enough, soon the skew was twisted in my hand and thrown against the work, where it dug out a chunk of wood. I was elated.

Chapter Six
MORTISING

Chair-making isn't brain surgery. An error of 1/32" in mortise placement won't bring the craftsmanship police to your door, although many makers of casework, equipped with machinist's measuring and layout tools, believe that it should. Instead, chair-making is a discipline of approximates, of things read by eye, a discipline still involving a hefty measure of intuition.

I'm not suggesting that anywhere-in-the-neighborhood is close enough, but on a practical level what happens is this: As a craftsman achieves more and more experience in the discipline, he realizes that chair-making is a pretty forgiving process. If the side rungs meet the back post at 99 degrees rather than 100 degrees, the chair will still come together. If a slat mortise is 1/16" lower on one back post than is the matching mortise on the other post, the chair will still come together. If the bottom back rung mortise is 7/8" deep instead of the ideal one full inch, the chair will still come together, even if the tenon is visible outside the post.

And no one will ever notice these errors.

True, those same imperfections might be glaring on a piece of Krenovian casework, but that's because on a piece by James Krenov, one of the most meticulous of contemporary woodworkers, there are so many straight-and-true reference lines with which the viewer can make comparisons. On a chair, however, everything is bent or tapered or joined at non-right angles, and in such a freewheeling environment the eye—even the educated eye—can't make accurate judgments.

I believe it's important that anyone approaching the discipline understand the difference between building a chair that is generally correct and building a chair that is perfectly correct. A generally correct chair can have all the structural qualities that will ensure a long, useful life. Its tenons can fit tightly into its mortises. Its posts can have a higher moisture content than its rungs, allowing for a fair amount of shrinkage. A generally correct chair can also be aesthetically pleasing. Its parts can be combined and shaped in such a way as to bring pleasure to the eye and comfort to the body of the beholder. The generally correct chair is not a perfect chair. It can still be, however, a completely successful chair.

LAYOUT (STORY) STICKS

Before I begin the construction of any chair, I sit down with the measured drawing, a try square, and a half dozen thin strips of hardwood that are at least 48" long to prepare my layout sticks. These allow me to mark the lengths and divisions of all posts and rungs without the drudgery and inherent inaccuracy of freehand measurement.

I begin by marking each end, the overall length of each turned piece. For the rungs, this includes the ⅞" long tenons on each end. I then mark the tenon shoulders.

The layout sticks for the posts are a little more complicated. On one side, I mark the centers of the mortises for the rungs on one face of the chair. Then I flip the stick over and mark the mortises for the rungs on the adjacent face of the chair. This means that each chair requires two post layout sticks: one for the front posts and one for the back posts. Also marked are the divisions for any post turnings.

I complete my preparations by making patterns for any band-sawn shapes (slats, arms, rockers) the chair might require.

MAKING THE POSTS

Chair-making begins and ends with the posts. Everything else—making the smaller parts, applying finishes, weaving seats—can be learned very quickly. And failure in the execution of these skills rarely involves any risk to the life of the chair. After all, if I foul up the weave on a chair seat, I just take the weave apart and reweave. That might take a bit of time, but it doesn't threaten the existence of the chair. And the same applies to the making of slats, arms, and rockers. These parts are simple to discard, easy to replace.

But the posts, particularly the back posts, are different. A completed back post that has been turned, sanded, marked, and given a finial represents a significant investment of time and materials. If, at assembly, a mistake in post manufacture is discovered, the entire chair-making process grinds to an ugly halt while new post material is located. Then again this material has to be ripped out, centered, turned, marked, and mortised.

MARKING MORTISE LOCATIONS ON THE POSTS

Although the process of marking mortise locations along the lengths of the posts is relatively straightforward, it's more difficult to mark them correctly on the circumference of the posts. And while there are shortcuts to this process, they almost always involve a high risk of failure. Even though the jigs discussed in the following pages take some time to construct, I think they are worth every minute to someone who's serious about making post-and-rung chairs.

Two methods are described below and in the accompanying pages. I've successfully used both methods in the construction of many chairs.

MARKING METHOD #1

The first method requires a lathe with an indexing head, which is a disk centered on the lathe's axis that has been divided into 36 equal segments. Each of these segments is marked by a hole drilled

through the disk near its outside diameter. A spring-loaded pin can be released into those 36 holes, locking the lathe at each position. This device allows the lathe operator to divide any turned form into 10-degree increments, each of the stops representing 10 degrees of the form's 360-degree whole.

After the posts are turned and sanded but before they're taken from the lathe, they must be marked for the drilling of the mortises.

All the post-and-rung chairs in this book involve the use of one of two sets of angles. The reproductions of Shaker production chairs (and the variations of those chairs that I've designed) have side rungs meeting the back posts 97½ degrees from the back rungs, while the side rungs meet the front posts at the supplementary angle of 82½ degrees from the front rungs. The remaining chairs—the transitional Mt. Lebanon rocker is one example—have side rungs meeting the back posts 100 degrees from the back rungs, while the side rungs meet the front posts at the supplementary angle of 80 degrees from the front rungs.

Front Posts

To mark the 80-degree angle between the front and side rungs on the front posts of the Mt. Lebanon transitional rocker, I remove the toolrest and position my line-marking gauge on the top of the lathe table. I then release the pin into one of the holes on the indexing head, taking care that the most attrac-

tive plain-sawn face of the post will be looking out from the finished chair in a direction that is 140 degrees from the front rung mortise. (Aligning the posts in this way not only displays the post's most attractive face, it also puts both the side rung tenons and the front rung tenons into positions that subject each to an equal amount of mortise shrinkage as the post dries.)

Bringing the pencil point of the line-marking gauge into contact with the post, I draw a line along the length of the post. One set of rung mortises will be drilled along this line. Then, using the spring-loaded pin to count stops on the indexing head, the work is turned eight positions, moving away from the best plain-sawn face. There I draw another line along the length of the post. The other set of rung mortises will be drilled along this second line.

When setting up the first line on each of the front posts (and later on, each of the back posts), it's important to remember that each pair of posts will have a right and left member. Briefly, this means that if the work is loaded into the lathe with the foot of the post toward the tail stock (my method) and the first line marks the front rung mortises (again, my method), stops on the indexing head will be counted clockwise on one post and counterclockwise on the other.

Back Posts

The method for laying out the mortise lines on the back posts differs from that for the front posts in two ways. First, the back rungs are set at a 100-degree angle to the side rungs. This means ten stops rather than eight on the indexing head. Also, to keep the post's most attractive plain-sawn face on the front side of the chair, I set the line for the back rungs so that the centerline of that face is 50 degrees forward of the line.

Once the lines are drawn that marking the placement of the mortises on the post's circumference, I mark off the divisions along the length of the post. To do this, I place my layout stick on edge along the line and, with a pencil, mark the center of each mortise. Then, flipping my layout stick over, I mark the centers of the mortises on the post's other line.

Marking and Cutting Mortises in Back Posts with Steam-Bent Slats

The following discussion applies only to chairs having steam-bent slats. Unbent slats, like those above the back panel on the Bubble-Slat Rocker (in the Contemporary Post-and-Rung Chairs section of projects in Chapter Nine), are centered on the same centerline as the rungs.

The rung mortises on the back ladder are made in exactly the same way as those on the front ladder. The slat mortises, however, require a different method. After drilling the rung mortises on the back posts, I steam-bend the posts. Then, after the posts have cured, the slat mortises can be chopped.

One at a time, these back posts are clamped to my bench top with the back rung centerline facing up. I then lay out the slat mortises, marking their widths and heights with a knife. Although the rungs at the base of the back ladder are set directly on the centerline made by the marking gauge, the slat mortises are set just a bit to the back of that centerline since they are steam-bent to conform more closely to the shape of the human back and therefore enter the back posts in a slightly different posture. *(See the drawing at right.)*

More specifically, I lay out the slat mortises so that their centerline is approximately 10 degrees behind the centerline of the rung mortises. Then I chop out the mortises, periodically checking their alignment by comparing a test-fit slat to a rung dry-fit into the bottom rung mortise

The preparation sequence for the back posts is as follows:

1. *Turn and mark the post.*
2. *Drill rung mortises.*
3. *Steam and bend back posts.*
4. *Chop slat mortises.*
5. *Assemble chair.*

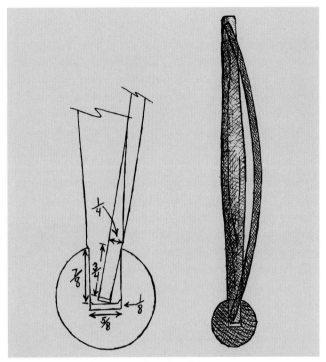

This drawing shows the details of the rung mortises and the slat mortises. Notice the ⅛" glue reservoir at the bottom of each. Notice, too, the slight shoulder above the rung tenon.

Remember that not all slat mortises are ⅞" deep. Those housing slats numbers 1 and 2 are shallower because those mortises are cut where the post diameter is less than the diameter of the post where the bottom mortises are cut.

The drawing illustrates the correct postures of rungs and steam-bent slats in the back ladder. When chopping a set of back-slat mortises, I put a reference rung in position in the bottom mortise of the back post. I check the progress of the slat mortises by periodically sighting past the bottom rung to the test-fit slat.

Because the slat mortises would weaken the upper—bent—portion of the back posts during the bending process, the slat mortises can't be chopped until the bends have been made; however, since a bent post won't fit securely against the fence on the rung mortising jig, I drill the rung mortises prior to bending.

Marking and Cutting Mortises in the Posts

Left: After locking the indexing head, I place the line-marking gauge on the lathe table. (If your lathe bed is made of angle iron, the gauge can be placed directly on the bed.) The point of the pencil is brought into contact with the front post. Then, maintaining that contact, I slide the point along the length of the post, creating a line that locates the post mortises on one face of the chair post.

Middle: Rotating the work eight stops on the lathe's indexing head brings the pencil point to a position 80 degrees from the first line. I then make a line along that point of the post's circumference, locating the post mortises on the adjacent face.

I place the layout stick on the post, aligning its foot with the foot of the post. Then, with a pencil, I mark the locations along that line on which the rung mortises will later be drilled. (On the back posts, these marks are made with a pen so that the steaming process won't obliterate my marks.)

Bottom: Both of my mortising jigs require a flat wood table, which I've bolted to the drill press's cast-metal table. The primary components of the front and back mortising jig (FRMJ) are the fence and the sliding carriage, which moves from right to left under the drill bit.

At this time, I set the height of the drill press table so that when the bit is brought down to its lowest point, it cuts a mortise that is 1" deep. This is the depth required for the ⅞" long tenons used on most of the chairs in this book. (The extra ⅛" is a glue reservoir so that the hydraulic pressure of the glue doesn't prevent the tenon from becoming fully seated.)

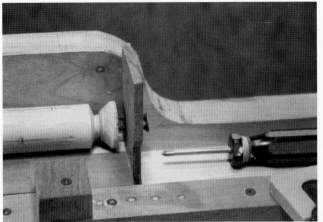

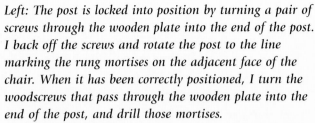

Left: The post is locked into position by turning a pair of screws through the wooden plate into the end of the post. I back off the screws and rotate the post to the line marking the rung mortises on the adjacent face of the chair. When it has been correctly positioned, I turn the woodscrews that pass through the wooden plate into the end of the post, and drill those mortises.

Middle left: I position the fence so that the distance between it and the lead point of the Forstner bit is half the diameter of the post being mortised. In this case the post has a diameter of 1⅜".

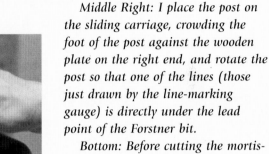

Middle Right: I place the post on the sliding carriage, crowding the foot of the post against the wooden plate on the right end, and rotate the post so that one of the lines (those just drawn by the line-marking gauge) is directly under the lead point of the Forstner bit.

Bottom: Before cutting the mortises, I clamp the back post to the edge of the bench. A pair of bar clamps locks the entire jig in position.

After cutting the slats to length, I number them with #1 indicating the top slat and #4 indicating the bottom slat. Length is determined by measuring out toward both ends from a centerline established with a try square. The tenon lengths are different on each slat, the longest tenons being established on the bottom slats, which will be fit into the back posts where their diameter is greatest.

I insert a reference rung in the bottom rung mortise (this rung is visible in the extreme right of the photo). Periodically during the mortising process, I'll test fit a slat and, from the foot, sight along the length of the post, comparing the position of the reference rung with the position of the test-fit slat. I then correct any error in slat mortise angle.

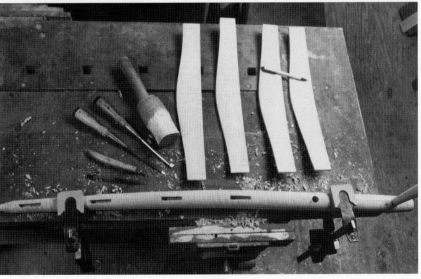

MARKING METHOD #2

After a couple of years of making chairs using Method #1, I felt that I needed different approach, a second method by which I could eliminate the troubling asymmetry in seat shape that was typical of chairs assembled in this way. This is how I came to develop the side rung mortising jig (SRMJ).

When I had first begun making chairs, I had built a table for my drill press that allowed me to hold back posts perpendicular to the axis of the drill bit as was described for the first mortising method. Setting the fence on this table so that it was half the diameter of the post from the lead point on the drill bit, I ran the bit down to the center point of each mortise. And while this method worked, it didn't produce mortises in a satisfactory alignment. Although the mortises were perpendicular to the length of the

post, it was very difficult to feed the lead point of my Forstner bit into the post dead-center on the line that marked mortise locations on the post's circumference. Any individual mortise might be several degrees out of alignment with the other mortises on that face of the chair.

Because of this I built my first jig—the front (and back) rung mortise jig: FRMJ, described in Method #1—with a carriage that allowed me to pass the post under the drill bit locked into a constant position relative to the circumference of the post. In practice I lay the post on the sliding carriage and adjust it so that the lead point of the Forstner bit hits the line drawn along the post's length. I then turn a couple of woodscrews through the wood plate on one end of the carriage into the end grain of the post's foot. I slide the carriage to the various locations along the post and drill the mortises.

It is, of course, possible to make errors when setting the post prior to fixing it in the carriage. However, what matters is that all of the mortises on that face of the chair are drilled in the same plane. In other words, it doesn't matter structurally whether that plane is precisely 80 degrees or 79 degrees from the plane of the adjacent face of the chair so long as the angle is consistent.

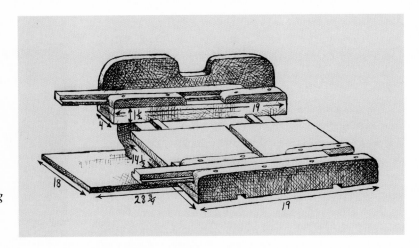

The exact dimensions of the side rung mortising jig (SRMJ) will be determined by the type of drill press being used and by the types of chairs being built. This drawing shows a few measurements that might help you get started in the construction of your own jig.

Notice that the tongued hardwood strips on which the posts will rest are elevated. This permits the chairs' back slats to bend down into the open space between the sliding hardwood strips during mortising.

▲▽▲▽▲▽▲▽▲▽▲▽▲▽▲▽▲▽▲▽▲▽▽

Setting up the Side Rung Mortising Jig (SRMJ)

Right, above and below: Like the previously discussed mortising jig, the SRMJ begins with the flat wooden table that I've bolted to the drill press's cast-metal table. Although it wasn't used in connection to the previous jig, the ¾" bolt that protrudes up through the wooden table is an essential part of the SRMJ.

I've screwed a small rectangle of plywood to the underside of the Baltic birch SRMJ table, which is fastened to a second rectangle of plywood via a hinge. A hole penetrates the second plywood rectangle, and a brass sleeve is fit into that hole and secured with silicon rubber. To install the SRMJ table, the brass sleeve is fitted over the ¾" bolt in the flat wooden table and the nut is turned down snug.

Left: This side view shows the angled SRMJ table supports. The angle is set so that the front and back chair ladders can be positioned under the drill bit at the correct angle that permits the accurate cutting of side rung mortises.

The angle of this jig allows me to drill the side rung mortises in chairs having angles of 82½ degrees between the front and side rungs and angles of 97½ degrees between the back and side rungs. By screwing wedges to the bottoms of the SRMJ table supports, I can change the angles to 100 degrees and 80 degrees. With the exception of the Shaker-style stool (on which all angles are 90 degrees), these two sets of angles are the only ones used on the chairs in this book.

Middle: The two bolts protruding from the SRMJ table in the previous photo are used to lock movable sliding tables into the correct positions for chair ladders of varying sizes. The hardware needed to install those bolts is shown here.

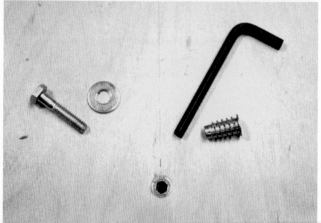

After drilling a hole into the SRMJ table, a deep-threaded metal insert (in the lower right quadrant of the photo) is turned into the Baltic birch, using an Allen wrench fit into the hexagonal lip of the insert. To fasten the sliding tables into position, I turn the machine bolt into the insert's machine threads—which begin below the hexagonal lip—drawing the bolt head snugly against the sliding table.

Bottom: The two sliding tables—one to support a ladder's right post and one to support the left—have dadoes cut into their bottom surfaces. These fit over hardwood strips screwed into matching dadoes cut into the SRMJ table.

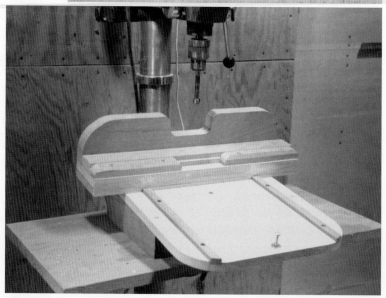

The back sliding table must be placed so that the hole bored by the Forstner bit is centered on the post's centerline. I sight from the end of the post up to the lead point of the bit. When they appear to be properly aligned, I tighten the machine bolt on the back sliding table and drill a mortise into a scrap post that has the same diameter as the post to be mortised. If the mortise is, in fact, centered in the scrap post, then I'm ready to begin mortising.

Details of the SRMJ

Top: This detail of the other side of the back sliding table shows the head of the machine bolt, which holds the back sliding table in the appropriate position.

Middle: This close-up shows one of the hardwood strips on which the sliding tables ride.

Bottom left and right: In both of the front and the back sliding tables, there is a tongued hardwood strip. These slide left and right under the drill bit to provide support for the posts of ladders that have been steam-bent.

These end views of the sliding strips in both the front and back sliding tables show the tongues that hold them in place.

Readying the SRMJ
for Mortising

Right: I've mounted the front sliding table, which, like the back sliding table, is held in position by tightening the machine screw into the threaded metal insert set into the SRMJ table.

Here the sliding hardwood strips in both the front and back sliding tables are clearly shown. The strips will support the partially assembled pieces.

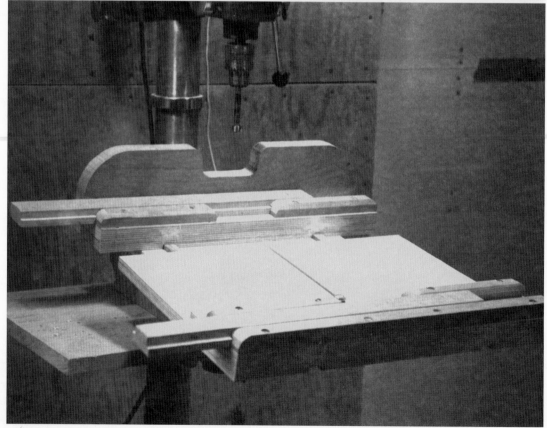

Bottom: The jig is set up for the drilling of side rung mortises in the back ladder.

For example, in this position, by sliding the strips to the left the strips will support a back ladder the bent ends of which extend to the right down into the gaps created in the surfaces of the front and back sliding tables.

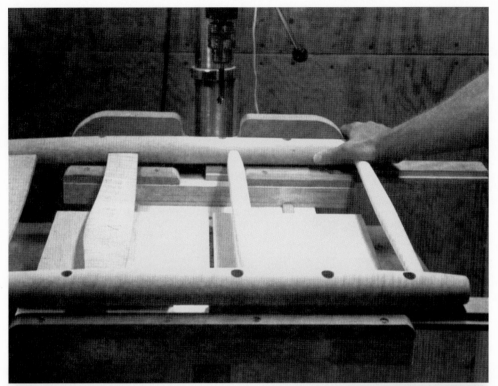

Positioning Work on the SRMJ

Left: In this photo I've positioned a back ladder for mortising. Notice that by sliding the tongued hardwood strips to the right, room has been created for the bent portions of the back posts on the left-hand side of the photo without losing a wide bearing surface for the posts during the mortising process.

Bottom: With this jig, I can quickly and accurately drill the side rung mortises for post-and-rung chairs.

Rotating the SRMJ to Mortise the Front Ladder

Left: Notice that in this photo the jig has been rotated on the ¾" bolt that protrudes up through the wooden table bolted to the drill press. To do this, both sliding tables must be removed and, after the SRMJ table is rotated, the sliding tables are placed into new positions on the SRMJ table.

With the jig in this position, I'm drilling the side rung mortises in the posts of the front ladder.

Bottom: The side rung mortises have been drilled into both the front and back ladders of this Mt. Lebanon #7 reproduction. Notice that the mortises drilled into the back ladder appear to be looking outward, while those drilled into the front ladder appear to be looking inward.

60

This first method of marking the angles between the front and side rungs and between the back and side rungs works well, and I used it for the construction of the first one hundred chairs I made. However, producing chairs with symmetrical seats using this method requires more accuracy than the human hand can routinely manage. This is because even the tiniest marking error on the circumference of the post is magnified along the length of the chair's rungs, and although all the chairs I've built with this method are structurally sound, a close inspection of their seat shapes reveals a perceptible asymmetry because, almost inevitably, the angles on one side of the seat are different than those on the other.

To remedy this, I stole a few ideas from John Alexander, some from Charles Harvey, and some from other chair-makers I had visited and read about. I began experimenting with a jig that would operate on a different principle. Instead of drilling all the rung mortises in the posts before assembling any part of the chair, I began, like many other chair-makers, to work out a two-part system. The two-part idea starts with partial assembly. The front and back ladders were assembled first (after the required mortises were marked and cut using the techniques described in Method #1). The troubling side rung mortises were then cut in a second step, with the aid of the SRMJ, into posts that were parts of these subassemblies.

What I found is that this method permits a much greater level of accuracy in the placement of the side rung mortises, eliminating perceptible seat asymmetry.

Chapter Seven
STEAM-BENDING

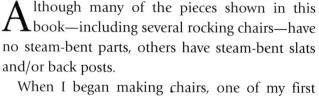

Although many of the pieces shown in this book—including several rocking chairs—have no steam-bent parts, others have steam-bent slats and/or back posts.

When I began making chairs, one of my first considerations was finding a low-cost method for generating the steam that bending requires. One method that's often cited in the woodworking press is built around a pan of water on an electric burner. The drawings of this arrangement are very clear—burner, pan of water, steam chamber of some sort. However, if this work is done in the kitchen (which is where most of us keep our electric burners), the steam produced would make humid swamps of our homes—peeling paint, loosening wallpaper, eroding marriages.

I searched for other possibilities.

A hot plate? Yes, it could be taken outside where the steam could rise harmlessly into the air; but the hot plates I found listed in the Sears catalog were anything but low-cost.

A pan of water over an open fire? It did offer the charm of being true to the centuries-old tradition of American chair-making. But it would be cumbersome to use on a regular basis.

What I wanted was something cheap, easy to construct (or adapt), and convenient to use.

Finally, in our laundry room, while looking for a clean pair of pants, I found the answer: a device my wife had picked up at a garage sale for $6. It was a 1500-watt, four-quart, deep-fat frier that I could fill with water, set at the appropriate temperature, and be rewarded with lots of steam.

To contain the steam, I bought a four-foot length of 4" PVC drainpipe. The salesman at the plumbing supply shop assured me that standard PVC would never stand up to the temperatures steaming would generate. His recommendation was cast-iron pipe at about four times the cost of PVC. I thanked him for his advice and bought the cheaper pipe.

To get the steam into the length of PVC, I cut a hole in the metal lid of the deep-fat frier that matched the outside diameter of the PVC. To hold the pipe above the surface of the water that I'd be boiling in the frier (so that I could collect all the steam that formed there instead of just that amount that formed within the 4" PVC), I turned four heavy-bodied sheet-metal screws—their sharp tips ground off to avoid scratching the materials I steamed—into the wall of the PVC about two inches above the bottom of the pipe. I left an inch protruding on the outside of the pipe wall to keep the bottom of the pipe from sliding too far through the hole cut in the frier's lid.

I considered several elaborate solutions to the problem of gasketing the narrow gap between the lid and the outside diameter of the PVC, then settled on duct tape, which holds up remarkably well, although it does require periodic renewal.

Because I was concerned that immersion might stain my wood, I screwed a piece of hardware cloth over the bottom end of the PVC, holding it in place with sheet-metal screws turned into the pipe. I now believe, however, that it probably doesn't make much difference; I suspect that the steamer would work just as well if the bottoms of the posts and slats stood in the water being heated by the frier.

At the plumbing supply shop I bought a cap to contain the steam in the pipe. Into this cap, I drilled a dozen ⅛" holes. Without these holes, the steam searches for and finds routes of escape (for instance around the frier's lid) that don't pass over the parts being steamed. The holes encourage a flow of steam up the length of the pipe.

It isn't pretty, but the entire apparatus sets up in less than five minutes, breaks down easily, and works every time. I should point out, however, that the plumbing supply salesman was right. The pipe has wilted a little, although not enough to interfere with the my ability to steam chair parts.

In this photo, I'm loading a set of chair slats into my steamer. Notice that the length of PVC passes through the deep-fat frier's metal lid. Notice, too, the hardware cloth that laps the bottom of the PVC.

The lid with the holes prepared in it has been placed on the deep-fat frier, and the PVC is held erect via a strip of wood lath screwed to the PVC and spring-clamped to the ladder.

Steam can be seen rising from the relief holes in the cap atop the length of PVC.

The entire apparatus sets up quickly and is assembled from inexpensive parts. And the best part about this odd-looking contraption is that it works every time.

BENDING FORMS

The second bit of hardware required by the steam-bending process is a set of bending forms. These have assumed thousands of different configurations over the years, and no single design is "best." In fact, anything that can hold steamed parts in the correct alignment throughout the drying process will work. Traditionally, a set of forms might consist of nothing more than three short posts: two that lock the ends of the part being bent and a third that positions the middle in such a way as to force a bend.

After experimenting with several sets of forms, I've settled on a set designed around three pipe clamps. These provide graceful bends without the strain of muscling freshly steamed parts into a stationary form. I place the freshly steamed parts between the shaped wooden jaws of the form and tighten the pipe clamp screws until the jig's two wooden jaws have forced the steamed parts into the correct alignment.

ALIGNING MATERIAL IN THE BENDING FORMS

The gradual bends required by the chairs in this book can be attained, for the most part, without giving much thought to the alignment (in relation to the annual rings) of the material in the bending forms. If the stock is straight-grained and without structural defects, the material is very forgiving and will permit the chair-maker to align the material in a manner that best suits his or her aesthetic goals. As I pointed out in Chapter Six, describing the marking of the lathe-mounted post stock, I align

my posts in a way that will ultimately present their best plain-sawn faces to a viewer standing in front of the chair. This method also aligns the post stock in a way that works best with the steam-bend required by many of the back posts. That is, it aligns the back posts so that the bend is nearly perpendicular to the posts' annual rings.

THE BENDING PROCESS

▲ Reference books suggest that, prior to bending, wood be steamed for an hour for each inch of its thickness.

I usually exceed this, especially when bending ¼" thick chair slats. These are always steamed for a minimum of thirty minutes.

▲ Only straight-grained pieces bend well and retain strength after bending.

A set of chair slats can be seen drying in my bending forms. The two bottom clamps are fit through openings in the forms' wooden jaws. The third clamp, on the top of the forms, is added to help keep the jaws perpendicular to the bottom edges of the slats. A separate set of curved wooden jaws with a different shape is used when drying a set of steamed back posts.

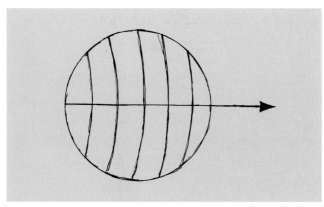

In this drawing, the post stock is shown in cross section to reveal the annual rings. Notice that the direction of the bend is perpendicular to the alignment of the rings. Although gradual bends can be made a bit to the right or left of a line perpendicular to the rings, sharp bends are best aligned in this manner.

This means that the grain must be continuous from end to end. Parts are likely to fracture wherever there is grain runout.

▲ Some woods bend better than others.

But I haven't yet found one that refuses to bend at all. In my experience, ash is the premier material for sharp bends. In fact, when building tape-back chairs from cherry or maple, I always bend the top and bottom tape bars from ash. The wood is covered by tape and so doesn't show, and ash can take the relatively sharp bends required by these tape bars without fracturing.

For the modest radii required by back posts, cherry, maple, and walnut all work very nicely. Also, when planed to a thickness of ¼", almost any wood can be bent into slats.

▲ Forms should exaggerate the desired shape.

There is always a certain amount of spring-back; however, the exact amount of necessary exaggeration is difficult to predict. Experimentation should be your guide.

▲ Parts bent once can be rebent.

Many times I've pulled a chair slat from the form to find its shape slightly distorted. Another round in the steam chamber and the drying form usually corrects this.

▲ How long should steamed parts remain in the drying form?

I'm not sure. In my shop I try for a week, although in a pinch I have pulled parts from the form after only three days— without disastrous consequences.

Chapter Eight
WEAVING SEATS

Most of the benches and stools appearing in this book have solid board seats; however, all the post-and-rung chairs are seated with material that has been woven over the seat rungs. Also, there are a number of chairs and settees with back panels similarly constructed of woven material.

The two Pilgrim chairs have seats woven of rush, which is made from the dried leaves of the cattail plant found growing in roadside ditches all over the country; and this is the one type of seating material I don't weave in my shop. Those chairs were sold unseated (and unfinished) and taken by the customer to a man specializing in distressed finishes, then on to a woman who weaves seats from rush. If you're interested in learning how to weave this beautiful and durable seating material, you can find several good books on the subject in your local library or bookstore.

On the other hand, the other two types of seating material appearing on the post-and-rung chairs—splint and Shaker tape—I do weave. This chapter will focus on the use of those materials.

SPLINT

I spent 8½ hours weaving my first rattan splint chair seat. Maybe three of those hours were actually spent weaving. Another hour was spent puzzling out the pattern, and the remaining hours were spent repeatedly reweaving areas I'd bungled. But I did learn, and by the time I had woven the third or fourth chair seat, I'd improved to a more respectable two hours per chair.

Traditionally, chairs of this type are seated with the inner bark of the hickory tree or with ash splint, which is obtained by pounding wet ash logs so that the grain separates and can be peeled away in narrow strips of loosened wood. Both are excellent seating materials, but both are expensive to buy and difficult to harvest on your own. Rattan splint, which is taken from the same plant that produces caning material, is readily available in consistently high quality at reasonable prices from mail order suppliers. For me, this combination of virtues is irresistible.

Rattan splint comes tied in bundles called hanks, in a variety of widths. To do a seat on an average chair, two to three hanks of ½" splint are required. The seat on a large chair (e.g., the Mt. Lebanon #7) requires a bit more, and the seat on a small chair (e.g., the two-slat side chair, the second project in the section of Shaker-style chairs in Chapter Nine, The Projects) requires a bit less.

Only a handful of tools are used in the process of weaving splint: scissors, a stapler, needlenose pliers, a butter knife, a spring clamp, a pencil, a couple of strips of sturdy tape (Scotch or masking tape will not do), and a bathtub.

As it comes from the supplier, splint is too brittle to be worked. It must first be soaked in a tub of warm water for an hour and a half to make it supple enough to weave.

While the splint is soaking, I lay out a rectangle on the chair's seat rungs. First, I measure the distance between the two back posts and subtract that distance from the distance between the two front posts. On the front seat rung, I put a mark that is half of that difference measured from the inside of one front post. Then I put a mark that is the same distance from the inside of the other front post. These two points, along with the inside edges of the back posts, enclose a rectangle that will be the first part of the seat to be woven.

If you look closely at an individual strand of splint, you notice that one surface has lifted fibers, while the other is harder and smoother. The smoother side goes up; the frayed side down, facing the rungs. Notice that the fibers have a grain, all lifting in the same direction. If you weave against the grain, you can damage or destroy your weaver.

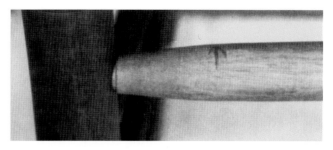

This pencil mark on the front rung indicates the front left corner of the rectangle that will be wrapped with the warp strands. Measured from the near post, the mark aligns with the inside of the back post.

The beginning of the first strand is taped to the side seat rung. A spring clamp is used to hold the warp in place while a new warp strand is attached to the end of the first warp strand with three staples located along an eight-inch lap.

When the warp has filled approximately half the area to be seated, a 1" foam cushion cut to the contour of the seat is slipped between the warp layers. This cushion helps the woven splint maintain its shape. Additional warp is then wrapped around this cushion.

When the splint has softened, I remove one hank from the tub and open it. The warp (this term denotes the splint that wraps the seat from front to back) is laid out first. In order to minimize the number of splices (which can later obstruct the weaving), I select the longest pieces of splint for the warp. Sometimes, if I'm dealing with a poor batch of splint, two or three hanks have to be opened to get enough long stuff to form the warp.

I begin by taping one end of the first strip to the inside of the right (my right when facing the chair, which is turned upside down) side seat rung, near the point at which that rung enters the mortise on the front post. (Most books will tell you to fasten that first strip with a furniture tack. Don't do this; it will crack the rung.) I then run that strip over the back seat rung just inside the post. Next, I pass the warp to the front seat rung, lapping it from underneath just to the left of the mark made on the front seat rung. The warp continues, returning to the back seat rung, over the rung, back to the front seat rung, until a point is reached at which insufficient length remains on that strand of splint to complete another circuit.

At this time, I splice on a new length of splint, taking care that the harder, smoother surface is on the face side. To make a splice, eight inches of the new strand are lapped over the last eight inches of the old. The strands are then fastened together with three staples.

I need to mention two points about the splices: First, all splices must take place on the underside of the chair. This restriction makes it is necessary to cut and discard some splint. Second, the staples should be set so that their prongs are folded over on the inside of the splint. This makes it possible to remove the staples with needlenose pliers once the weaving is complete—something I don't bother with on the seats, but something that is necessary on the backs.

The first weaver doesn't wrap around the side seat rungs. Instead, both ends are tucked under warp strands on the top surface of the seat. The function of the first weaver is simply to fill in the space between the back posts.

This detail shows one end of the first weaver being tucked under a strand of the warp. Notice the weaver's pattern. It crosses over three strands of warp, then under three strands of warp.

Splices are made in the weaver by lapping the first six or eight inches of a new strand over the last six or eight inches of the old strand. Although some books indicate that these splices should be made only on the bottom side of the seating material, I splice on both the top and bottom surfaces to avoid wasting splint.

When the weavers have filled approximately half the distance to the front seat rung, the gussets (the triangular areas to the right and left of the rectangle formed by the warp) can be filled in with short strips woven back into the weave, then tucked under at the ends. These strips then pass over the front seat rung and are similarly woven into the weave on the bottom side of the seating material.

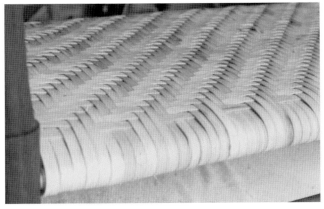

One way to check the accuracy of the weave is to sight the diagonals. Any error is quickly apparent.

Approaching the midway point of the warp, I feed a 1" foam cushion cut to the shape of the seat between the layers of warp. This softens the sitting a bit, but primarily the purpose of the cushion is to give the seat "body," so that the splint doesn't become loose and sag.

I continue wrapping the warp around the rungs until I've completely covered the length of the back seat rung. Finally, the end of the last strand of warp passes over the front seat rung from above and is taped to the side rung near the back post.

At this point, I'm ready to begin weaving. The first weaver (the splint that runs from side to side) fills the space between back posts. Unlike the other weavers, it doesn't wrap around the side rails to the underside of the chair. One end of this weaver is loosely folded over—two or three inches would be enough—and hooked under the second (counted from either side) strand of warp. Then it alternately passes over three and under three strands until it reaches the other back post. At this point it is cut off, leaving two or three inches to fold over.

The second weaver begins on the underside of the chair. On a padded surface, I turn the chair over and begin feeding one end of the weaver into the warp just forward of the two back posts. As it is throughout the weaving process, the pattern here is "over three and under three," and so on across the chair bottom. When the weaver has reached the opposite side, I turn the chair over so that it's upright and begin weaving across the top side of the warp using the free end of the weaver. It's important to understand this particular twill pattern.

Take a moment to study the photos. Notice how the beginning of each successive row of weave is staggered over one warp row. For example, this second row of weave enters the warp one strip behind the point at which the first weaver enters the warp. Both then revert to the standard "under three and over three" pattern.

When I reach the opposite side of the chair, I draw the weaver tight, turn the chair over, and begin weaving with the free end of the weaver across the bottom of the chair. Here, too, I stagger the weaver's entrance to the warp just as was done on the top side of the chair, continuing in this manner until I run out of weaver.

Then I splice on a new piece. To splice weavers, no staples are used. I simply weave the first eight inches of the new weaver over the last eight inches of the old. The tightness of the weave holds the joint in place. It is, in fact, this tightness that holds our weight when we sit in these chairs.

When the weave has reached two-thirds of the way to the front seat rung, I begin weaving the gussets. These are the triangular areas to the right and left of the rectangle covered by the warp. I pull the end of the first warp strip free from the tape that holds it to the left side rail. Then, following the already established twill pattern, I feed this strip into the weavers, hooking the end over one of the weavers near the rear of the seat. On the bottom side, I do the same with the taped end of the last warp strip.

The remainder of the gussets are filled in with short strips fed into the weave on both the top and bottom of the seat in the same manner as the end of the first warp strip. In order to have a seat that is strong in the gussets, I feed these short strips as far back into the weave as possible, loosely hooking the ends of each over a strip of weave.

When all the gusset strips are in place, I continue weaving. These last few weavers can be difficult to get into place as tightness accumulates, approaching the front seat rung. A point is reached at which I can no longer feed the weavers through the warp with my fingers. At that point, I use a butter knife laid under the warp strips as a guide for the weavers and, at the very end drag the weaver along its course with a pair of needlenose pliers.

This photo shows a settee frame that is ready to have the seat and back panel woven.

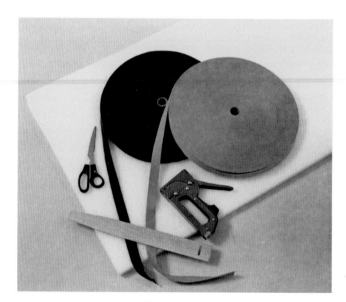

Weaving tape requires few tools. Notice the flat wooden weaving needle at the bottom of the photo. The end of the weaver is passed through the opening, and then taped into place.

To start, one end of the warp for the settee's back panel is stapled to the back underside of the top frame rung.

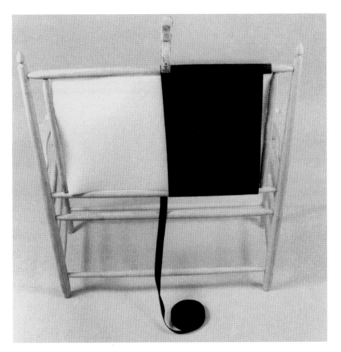

The foam cushion is inserted when the warp has covered about half of the back panel.

These seats can be finished with a mixture of equal parts boiled linseed oil and mineral spirits. This keeps the splint supple and makes it easier to wash dirt from the seat. Recently, I've been using the same finish on the seats that I use on the wood surfaces of the chair: equal parts boiled linseed oil, mineral spirits, and polyurethane. The polyurethane appears to add an extra level of protection. And on some chairs, I've painted the seats after applying a coat of good primer.

SHAKER TAPE

Early in the nineteenth century, Shaker chair-makers began to move away from the splint seats that had so far appeared on most of their chairs, instead using a woven fabric tape often dyed in very bright colors. The very first tapes were woven by hand, usually of wool or perhaps wool in which a bit of linen or cotton was mixed. Today, a similar tape is widely available to chair-makers from a number of mail order sources. This tape is machine-woven of cotton dyed in a variety of colors, and although it's much easier to weave than splint, it is also much more expensive.

Typically, the material is woven in a checkerboard pattern, the weaver going under one strand of warp, then over the next, and so on. Quite often, this pattern is reinforced by using one color for the warp and a second for the weave. Even fewer tools are needed for weaving tape than for the weaving of splint. A pair of scissors and a stapler loaded with ¼" staples are the only essentials, although I also have a wide wooden weaving needle that can make the seating process move a bit more quickly.

I prefer staples to furniture tacks for attaching the tape to the chair frame. Staples are thin and penetrate easily without damaging the wood whereas tacks have much thicker shanks that can crack the rungs.

Tape, unlike splint, is available in 75-yd rolls, which means that the splicing process is all but eliminated. (Sometimes, at the ends of rolls, it will be necessary to splice. In such a case a needle and some sturdy thread are employed.) However, since it's very difficult to pass a 75-yd roll between the strands of the warp, I begin by estimating the necessary length of tape for the warp and the weaver, cutting those portions from the roll to simplify the handling of the material.

I begin weaving a tape back—which is exactly the same as weaving the area of the seat between the gussets—by attaching the lead end of the warp to the back side of the top tape frame rung with a pair of ¼" staples. I then pass the warp over the top tape frame rung and down over the front of the bottom tape frame rung. Next, I bring it up to the top frame rung, where it is then aligned with the first course of tape.

Then, I begin the second course of the warp. When about half of the back panel is wrapped , I insert a 1" foam cushion. Although the cushion doesn't seem to add much comfort to the seat of a chair bottomed with splint, it adds considerably to the comfort of one bottomed with tape. Plus it keeps the tape taut, permanently maintaining the smooth look and feel of a newly woven seat.

Next, I begin passing the weaver through the warp. Stapling one end of the weaver to the back inside surface near the bottom of one of the false back posts, I wrap the weaver around that back

The seat gusset strips are put in place once the weaving has reached about halfway to the front seat rung. The gussets are cut to length and then woven into the weavers. These strips are then stapled into place, care being taken that the staples are hidden underneath the strands of the weaver.

It took me about four hours to weave the Shaker tape seat and back on this settee.

The weaving needle simplifies the process when the warp has tightened too much to pass a coil of tape between the strands. I tape the free end of the weaver to the flat wooden weaving needle and then use the needle to guide the weaver.

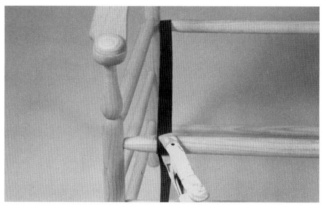

The seat is laid out for the weaving of tape in the same way as for the weaving of splint.

post, across the front of the back panel, alternately over and under each strand of the warp. This weaving process continues across the back.

I use two different methods for passing the weaver through the warp. First, early in the weaving process when there's a fair amount of slack, I'll pass a tightly wound coil of weaving material through the warp. Then later, as the warp begins to tighten, I tape the free end of the weaver to a flat wooden weaving needle to guide the weaver.

When the back panel has been fully woven, I staple the end of the weaver to the back inside surface of one of the false back posts. However, many seat weavers do not fasten that end, instead simply tucking it in under the last strand of the warp that it crosses—a method that seems to hold up very nicely.

Chapter Nine
THE
PROJECTS

Some of the projects appearing in this chapter are reasonably accurate reproductions of period or Shaker originals. For example, except for the choice of materials—cherry and curly maple—used in its manufacture, the little two-slat side chair is pretty faithful to a Shaker original drawn by John Kassay in *The Book of Shaker Furniture* (1980). Similarly, although I'm certain the exact measurements of my Brewster chair are different from those of the original, mine is nevertheless a reasonable likeness of one appearing in Wallace Nutting's 1928 *Furniture Treasury*.

But no chair in this book is an exact copy of any specific period or Shaker original. In many cases, these changes from the originals were dictated by my customers. For instance, although they might have wanted the general shape of a Mt. Lebanon transitional rocker, they might also have wanted a finial more like one found on a chair that their grandmother kept in her kitchen. Too, sometimes, they mixed and matched parts from so many sources that what resulted bore little resemblance to any historical original.

Also, some of the variations from period or Shaker originals are the result of my ignorance. One example of this can be found in the Shaker-style settee with tape seat and back. At the time I built it, I had seen only one grainy photo of a Mt. Lebanon original. I had no measurements, no photo close-ups; and, as a result, the settee differs from the originals in several important ways. First, the back posts on mine are not steam-bent, although I have since been told by knowledgeable students of Shaker furniture that those on the originals were. Second, the feet of the front posts of my settee lack the concave taper found on the originals. And third, it's my understanding that the originals were considerably bigger than mine, which I developed by taking the frame of a #5 and adding to its width.

Also, some of the changes from the originals are the result of my What if? mentality. What if I made the sweep on the arm of that #7 just a bit more dramatic? What if I made the mushroom caps flatter or taller? What if I used mixed woods? These changes from the originals were never intended to be improvements on those originals. (I'm not sure that would possible.) They are instead nothing more than the result of my perverse inclination to tinker.

Other chairs, although heavily influenced by Shaker forms, are my designs and so don't resemble anything found in any historical collection.

These do not comprise a collection of carefully researched historical designs. They do, instead, comprise a collection of designs that I have made in the shop to meet the demands of my customers and my imagination. Readers intending to make historically accurate chairs might use the methods discussed in this book to build reproductions based on drawings in Kassay's *The Book of Shaker Furniture* or on Ejner Handberg's excellent books of drawings.

Important Note: Unless stated otherwise, all tenons for all post-and-rung chairs will have a diameter of ⅝".

Windsor-Style Pieces

▲▽▲▽▲▽▲▽▲▽▲▽

A Windsor is defined as a chair or stool with a solid seat into which leg tenons (and in most cases back spindles) are mortised. Although none of the following pieces exhibit the complexity that is typical of first-rate Windsors, all do have leg tenons mortised into solid-wood seats, and all can serve as an introduction to the process of making Windsor chairs.

RUSTIC STOOL (sassafras and walnut)

Although very primitive in construction, this stool has a certain sprightly charm, and because of its long leg tenons passing through the thick seat

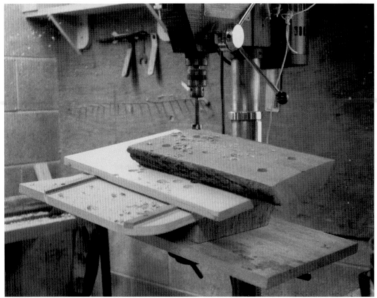

This photo shows the seat blank on the SRMJ (side rung mortise jig). Notice the two planes meeting at the axis of the drill bit, each having angles of 97½ degrees. One tilts to the photo right. The other tilts forward, perpendicular to the back of the drill press table, toward the photo's left.

stock, it is a piece that will take a good deal of abuse, even without the reinforcement of stretchers connecting the legs.

I cut the mortises for the leg tenons on the drill press using the SRMJ (side rung mortise jig) described in Chapter Six, Marking Method #2. Although designed to cut side rung mortises for post-and-rung chairs, this jig can be adapted to cut leg tenon mortises in solid-wood chair seats.

Because I wanted the legs to splay in two directions, after mounting the SRMJ on my drill press table I tilted the table 97½ degrees. This setup gave me the same angle in two planes: one parallel to the back of the drill press table (the angle created by tilting the table) and another perpendicular to the back of that table (the angle created by the SRMJ). Then, placing the stool's seat blank on the SRMJ with its bottom surface facing up, I drilled the four mortises.

RUSTIC STOOL (sassafras and walnut)

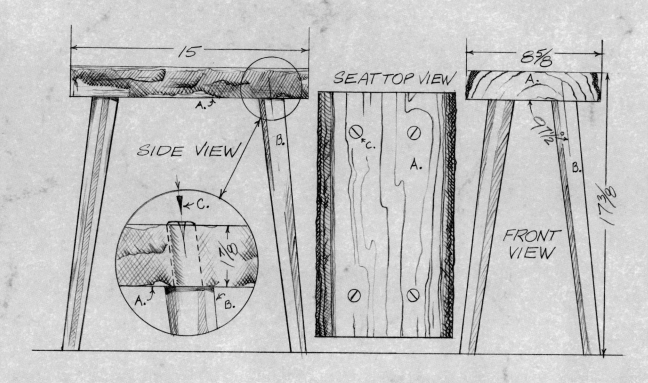

MATERIALS LIST

A Seat   1 pc.   1⅞ x 8⅝ x 15

B Legs   4 pcs.   1⅝ x 1⅝ x 17⅜ *

C Wedges   4 pcs.   ⅛ x ⅞ x ¾

* Leg tenons should be made ⅛" longer than is indicated by this finished leg length so that they can be pared smooth while still standing ¹⁄₁₆" proud of the bench top.

THREE-LEGGED STOOL
(sassafras and walnut)

I cut the mortises, in that end of the seat housing two leg tenons, exactly like those in the seat of the previously described stool (having splay in two directions). The mortise on the other end, however, was cut by aligning the seat's centerline midway between the planes having 97½-degree angles.

STOOL WITH SCULPTED SEAT
(cherry and ash)

Although this one is three-legged like the previous stool, I cut the leg tenon mortises using a slightly different method. In this case, I cut all three—including the tenon of the singleton leg—as if this were a four-legged stool. The result is that the stool has a different posture from the stool described on the left.

MATERIALS LIST

A	Seat	1 pc.	1¾ x 7½ x 13
B	Legs	3 pcs.	2 x 17 *
C	Wedges	3 pcs.	³⁄₁₆ x ⅞ x ¾

* Tenons should be made ⅛" longer than is indicated by this finished leg length so that they can be pared to match the surface of the seat.

MATERIALS LIST

A	Seat	1 pc.	3 x 8½ x 15¾
B	Legs	3 pcs.	1½ x 18½ *
C	Wedges	3 pcs.	³⁄₃₂ x ⅞ x ¾

* The leg on the right penetrates the surface of the seat and is then cut off and pared flush with the surface of the seat.

Three-Legged Stool (above) & Stool with Sculpted Seat (below)

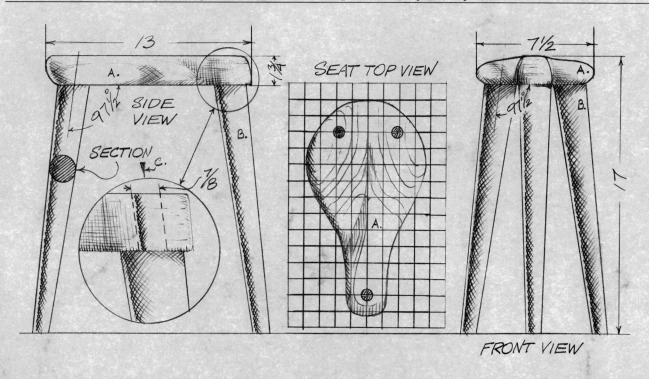

13

A.

3/4

97 1/2°

SIDE VIEW

SECTION

C.

7/8

SEAT TOP VIEW

A.

7 1/2

A.

B.

97 1/2°

17

FRONT VIEW

BOTH GRIDS 1 INCH

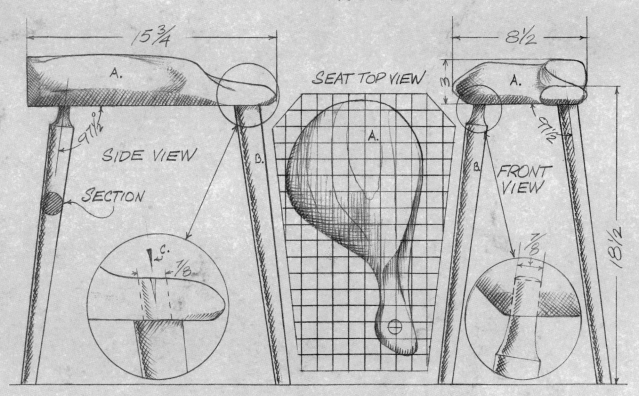

15 3/4

A.

97 1/2°

SIDE VIEW

SECTION

C.

1/8

B.

SEAT TOP VIEW

A.

8 1/2

3

A.

97 1/2°

B.

FRONT VIEW

7/8

18 1/2

79

WINDSOR STOOL WITH PAINTED SEAT (white oak)

I cut the mortises for the tenons atop each leg in the same way as the leg tenon mortises for the rustic bench described earlier.

With the drill press table returned to its normal position of 90 degrees from the axis of the drill bit, I cut the mortises in the legs for the side stretcher tenons. The angle for this joint is created by the 97½-degree angle created by the SRMJ.

The mortises for the center stretcher tenons were then cut using the jig described in Chapter Six, Marking Method #1, because these mortises enter the side stretchers 90 degrees from the axis of the side stretchers.

MATERIALS LIST

A Seat	1 pc.	1¾ x 11⅛
B Legs	4 pcs.	1¾ x 19⅞ *
C Side stretchers	2 pcs.	1½ x 8⅞ **
D Center stretcher	1 pc.	1½ x 9

* Includes a 1" tenon.
** Includes a 1" tenon on each end.

Note: The tenons at the top of each leg have a diameter of 1". The tenons at each end of the side stretchers have a diameter of ⅞". The tenons at each end of the center stretcher have a diameter of ⅝".

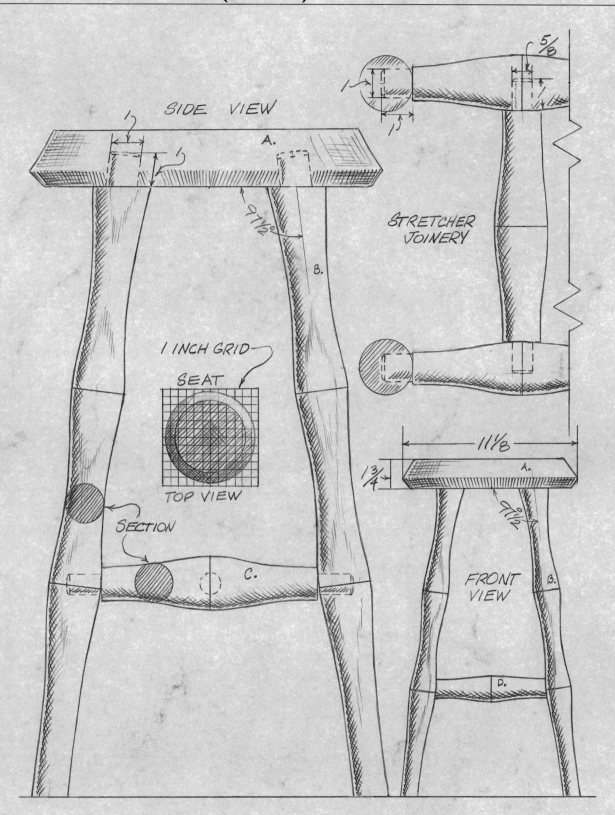

SIDE VIEW

A.

9'1½"

B.

1 INCH GRID

SEAT

TOP VIEW

SECTION

C.

STRETCHER JOINERY

5/8

11⅛"

1¾

A.

7½

FRONT VIEW

B.

D.

ZOAR-STYLE CHAIR (white ash)

This chair is patterned after several made by the Zoarites, members of a communal society flourishing in northeastern Ohio during the nineteenth century. Like much Zoarite furniture, the form can be traced to the society's Germanic origins.

After dimensioning the lumber, I turned the legs and band-sawed the rounded corners of the seat and the contours of the chair back. Then I installed all three cleats on the bottom of the seat, taking care to pass the screws through oversized holes in order to allow for the expansion and contraction of the seat in response to seasonal changes in relative humidity.

Next, using the method described for the drilling of the leg tenon mortises on the Rustic Stool, I drilled the four mortises for the leg tenons, working from the underside of the seat.

With a band saw and a backsaw, I formed the three ½ x 1½ x 2 tenons at the base of the chair back, leaving the shoulder at a 90-degree angle to the chair back's front and back faces.

I then laid out the mortises for the triple tenons. Placing the seat on the SRMJ with its top surface up (in the same position as that used in the cutting of the mortises for the leg tenons, tilting down toward the drill press operator), I cut three ⁷⁄₁₆" holes through the thickness of both the seat and the cleats underneath, aligning those holes within the limits of each of the three ½ x 1½ mortise locations.

The mortise angle this created allowed me to position the chair back in a comfortable posture.

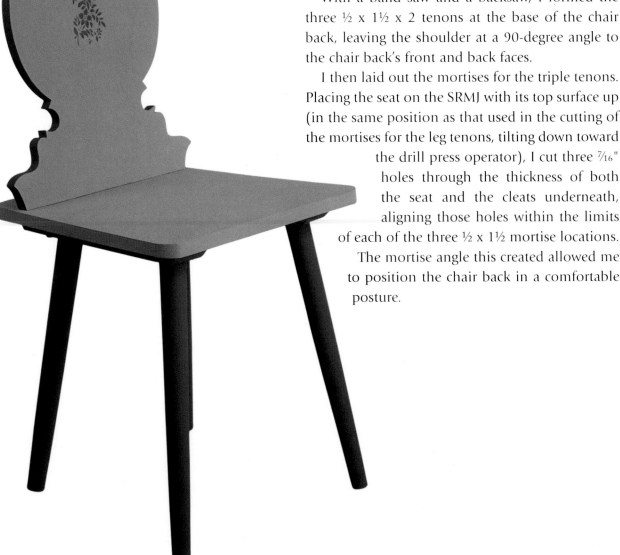

Then, working from both the top and the bottom, I defined the mortise walls with a paring chisel. Finally, with the tenons fully seated in their mortises so that the shoulder on the back face of the chair back was tight against the seat, I scribed a line across that back. The line was set a distance from the seat surface that was equal to the gap between that surface and the tenon shoulder on the front side of the seat back.

Then I pared the angle for that shoulder, joining the scribed line on the back to the sawn line on the front.

This photo shows the triple tenons at the base of the chair back. Although it may be hard to see, the shoulder is angled to sit tight against the seat surface when the tenons are fit into their mortises.

The angle of the chair back can be seen more easily in this photo.

This shot looks at the underneath of the seat of the Zoar-Style Chair, showing the triple tenons from the base of the chair back passing through both the seat and the cleats.

This chair poses some interesting design problems. Obviously, the grain in the seat must run perpendicular to the grain in the cleats, but if the legs penetrate both the seat and the cleats, the wood in the seat is prevented from expanding and contracting. I wonder how the Zoars solved this.

My solution? Although it may seem a little inelegant, my answer to this problem was to relieve, with a rasp, the front and back surfaces of the leg tenons where those tenons pass through the cleats. This should allow for some seasonal wood movement.

MATERIALS LIST

A	Seat	1 pc.	$^{13}/_{16}$ x $16^{11}/_{16}$ x $17^{3}/_{4}$
B	Back	1 pc.	$^{11}/_{16}$ x 16 x $19^{15}/_{16}$
C	Front legs	2 pcs.	$1^{1}/_{2}$ x $18^{3}/_{4}$ *
D	Back legs	2 pcs.	$1^{1}/_{2}$ x $17^{3}/_{4}$ *
E	Long cleats	2 pcs.	$^{7}/_{8}$ x $2^{3}/_{8}$ x $15^{1}/_{4}$
F	Short cleat	1 pc.	$^{7}/_{8}$ x $2^{3}/_{8}$ x $6^{1}/_{4}$
G	Wedges	4 pcs	$^{3}/_{32}$ x $^{7}/_{8}$ x $^{3}/_{4}$

* Includes a 2" tenon that is cut off and pared flush with the surface of the seat after assembly.

Zoar-Style Chair (white ash)

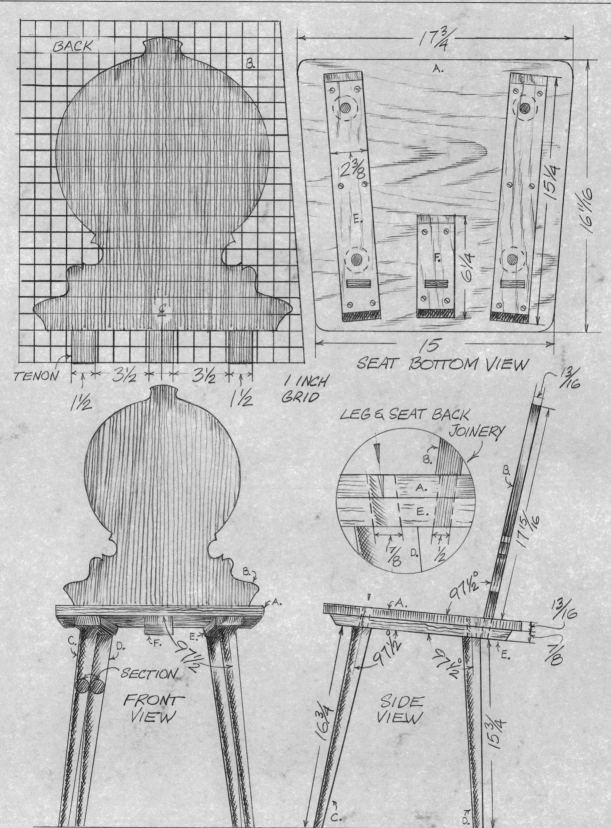

BACK

B.

TENON

1½   3½   3½   1½

1 INCH GRID

17¾

A.

2⅜

E.

F.

6¼

15¼

16¹¹⁄₁₆

15

SEAT BOTTOM VIEW

LEG & SEAT BACK JOINERY

B.

A.

E.

⅛   D.   ½

B.

13/16

B.

17¹⁵⁄₁₆

13/16

⅛

97½°

C.   D.   F.   E.

97½

SECTION

FRONT VIEW

A.

E.

97½

97½

16¾

SIDE VIEW

15¾

C.   D.

Benches

△▽△▽△▽△▽△▽△▽

The simple but functional four-board bench is an American classic. Consisting of a top, two ends, and a stretcher, this construction provides sturdy seating for a relatively minor investment of time and materials.

The two examples that follow were developed from several Shaker origi-nals. The first (pictured below) has joinery—a combination of dadoes and wedged through-tenons—taken from a bench made in the Shaker commu-nity at South Union, Kentucky, during the first half of the nineteenth cen-tury, an example drawn by John Kassay. Other features—size, leg shape, stretcher profile—were adapted from other Shaker examples.

The second bench—with wedged stretcher tenons—was developed after one drawn by Ejner Handberg.

Four-Board Bench (walnut)

FOUR-BOARD BENCH (walnut)

After band-sawing the curves on the top, the legs, and the stretcher, I cut the dado on the bottom face of the bench top. I find it easiest to use a table saw cut-off box for this operation, but it could also be done with a radial arm saw or a router.

The bulk of the mortise waste is removed with a drill bit. I then clean up the mortise walls with a chisel.

After cutting the through-tenons and the stretcher notch at the top of each leg, I mark the mortises on the bench top. First, the widths of the dadoes on the bottom face of the bench top must be squared around to the top face. Then, using the through-tenons at the top of each leg as guides, the width of the mortises is marked.

The various parts of the four-board bench seen prior to assembly.

At this stage, the parts are test-fit. Notice the X at the top of the leg and the corresponding X on the edge of the bench top. These marks ensure that at final assembly the bench comes together in the same alignment as it did during the test assembly. Once an accurate fit is established, I cut the V-shaped notches across the width of each through-tenon.

After applying glue to the various joint components and assembling the bench, I drive the wedges into their notches.

MATERIALS LIST

A	Bench top	1 pc.	¾ x 8¼ x 40
B	Legs	2 pcs.	¾ x 8¼ x 16 *
C	Stretcher	1 pc.	¾ x 3 x 34
D	Wedges	4 pcs.	¼ x 1⁵⁄₁₆ x 1

* Tenons should be made ⅛" longer than is indicated by this finished leg length so that they can be pared flush with the top after assembly.

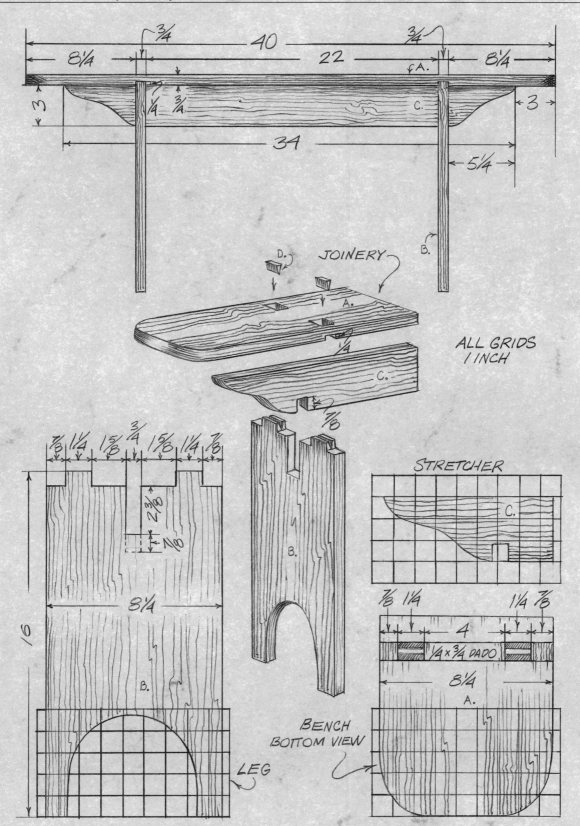

JOINERY

ALL GRIDS
1 INCH

STRETCHER

BENCH
BOTTOM VIEW

LEG

1/4 x 3/4 DADO

FOUR-BOARD BENCH
WITH WEDGED STRETCHER TENONS (curly maple)

Unlike the joinery described for the previous
bench, the wedged through-tenons on this example
weren't set into a dado. Notice, too, that on this
example the stretcher joinery was handled in the
same way as the leg joinery.

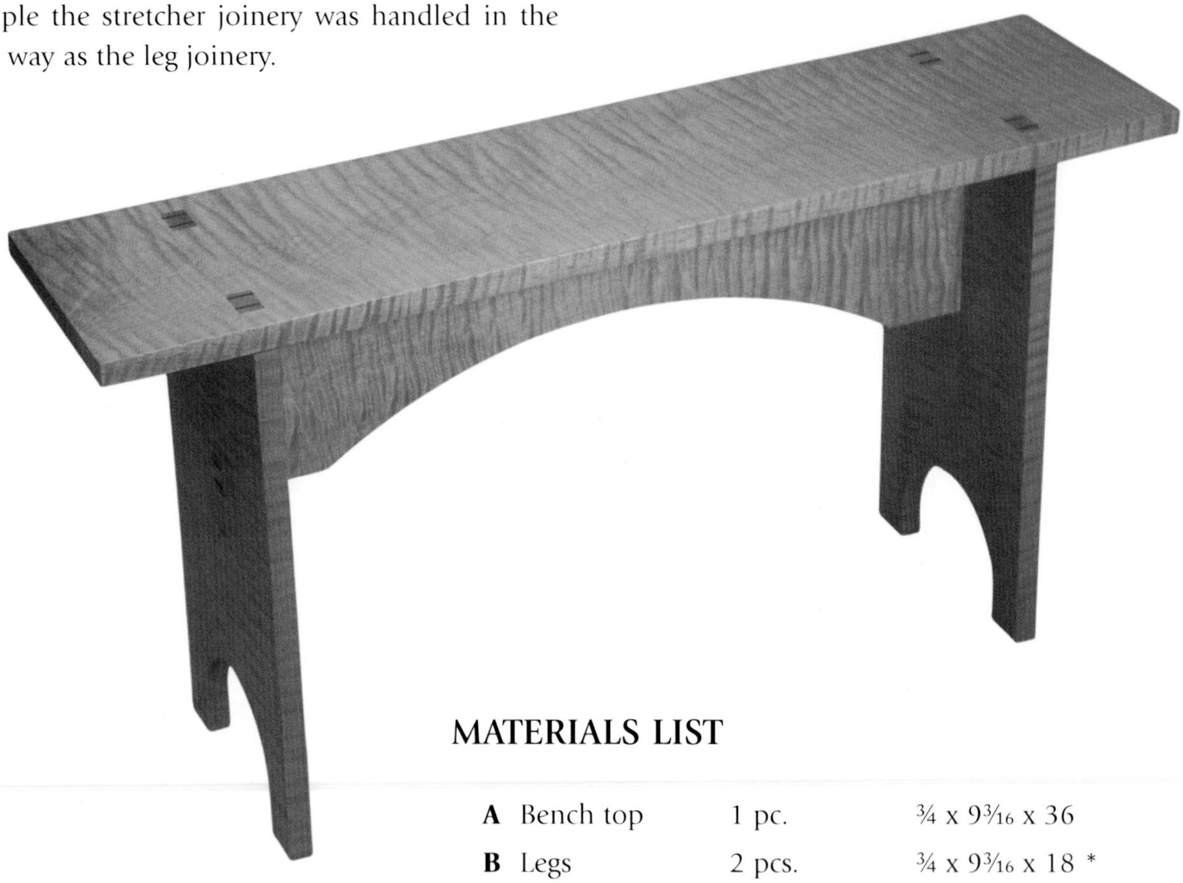

MATERIALS LIST

A	Bench top	1 pc.	¾ x 9³⁄₁₆ x 36
B	Legs	2 pcs.	¾ x 9³⁄₁₆ x 18 *
C	Stretcher	1 pc.	¾ x 6¾ x 27 *
D	Wedges	16 pcs.	³⁄₃₂ x ¾ x ¾

* Tenons should be made ⅛" longer than is indicated by this finished leg length so that they can be pared flush with the top and the
outside faces of the legs after assembly.

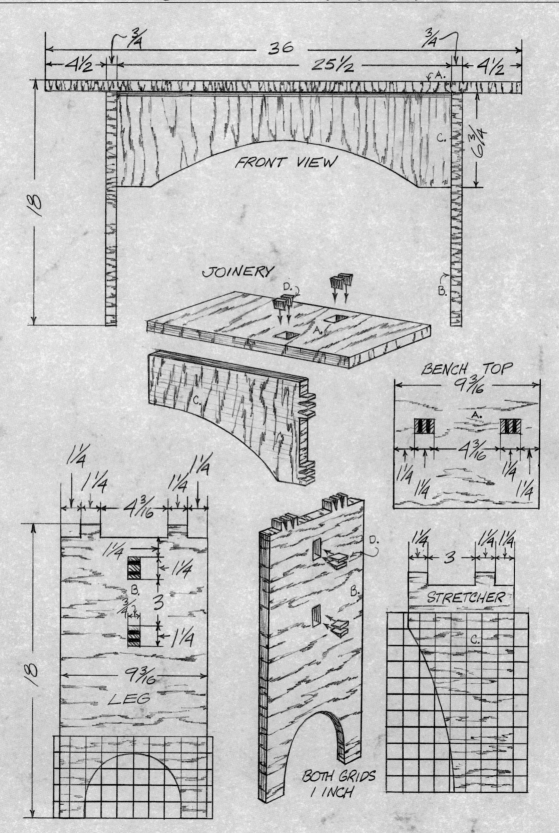

FRONT VIEW

JOINERY

BENCH TOP
9 3/16

LEG

STRETCHER

BOTH GRIDS
1 INCH

Shaker-Style Chairs

▲▽▲▽▲▽▲▽▲▽

The Shaker Chair *by Charles Muller and Timothy Reiman is an essential resource for any serious maker of post-and-rung chairs. Hundreds of different forms appear on its pages, not only those mass-produced in the Mt. Lebanon chair factories but also forms produced in other communities, made in far fewer numbers often for the exclusive use of the Shaker community's Brothers and Sisters.*

Typically, my customers have asked for chairs modeled after those built under the direction of R. M. Wagan of the Mt. Lebanon family, as these are the chairs that have received so much notice. But occasionally a more knowledgeable buyer has asked for something a little different, and it's then that I've turned to resources like The Shaker Chair.

What follows is a sampling of the Shaker-style chairs built in my shop: chairs based on originals produced by several different nineteenth-century Shaker communities.

CHAIR ARMS (tenoning & installation) ▲▽▲▽▲▽▲▽▲▽▲▽▲▽▲▽▲▽▲▽▲▽

Note: All chair arms are tenoned and installed in the same way. First the tenon (which is installed into the chair's back post) is formed by hand with a shop knife and a rasp, checking the diameter several times in a hole drilled into a test block.

Installation of the arm can be a little tricky. I stand the arm on its outside edge and feed the tenon into its mortise. Then, when that tenon is fully seated, I roll the arm up over the tenon atop the front post, tapping it with my soft mallet to bring it into its proper place.

STOOL WITH MULTICOLORED TAPE (cherry)

This stool consists of parts borrowed from a Mt. Lebanon #5: four front posts, six front rungs, and six side rungs—the side rungs being mortised into the posts 90 degrees from the front rungs on the stool's adjacent face.

As I did with the first hundred chairs that originated in my shop, I built this stool without the SRMJ described in Chapter Six, Marking Method #2. Instead, I located the mortises for the rungs on adjacent faces of the chairs by drawing two lines along the length of each post 90 degrees apart, measuring that distance by counting stops on my lathe's indexing head.

Then I fixed the post in the jig described in Chapter Six, Marking Method #1, and cut the mortises along one line—after which the post was rotated in the jig as fixed into place, and the mortises were cut along the other line.

Although when sighted from above, error can be seen in the angles at which the side rungs meet the front and back of the stool, this piece went together very nicely and would probably pass inspection from any except the most critical craftsman.

MATERIALS LIST

A	Posts	4 pcs.	1⅜ x 19³⁄₁₆
B	Long seat rungs	2 pcs.	1 x 19¾ *
C	Long rungs	4 pcs.	⅞ x 19¾ *
D	Short seat rungs	2 pcs.	1 x 16½ *
E	Short rungs	4 pcs.	⅞ x 16½ *

* Includes a ⅞" tenon on each end.

TWO-SLAT SIDE CHAIR (cherry and curly maple)

Ingenuity is one of the signature features of Shaker design. This two-slat side chair, for example, was created with a low back to permit the chair to be pushed completely under the table to simplify after-dinner cleanup. Although not perhaps as comfortable as chairs with a higher back, it is an eminently functional piece of dining-room furniture, suitable for use in the modern home.

Unlike the chairs already presented in this book, this example has steam-bent back slats.

MATERIALS LIST

A	Back posts	2 pcs.	$1\frac{7}{16}$ x $25\frac{1}{2}$
B	Front posts	2 pcs.	$1\frac{7}{16}$ x $17\frac{1}{8}$
C	Front seat rung	1 pc.	1 x $17\frac{3}{4}$ *
D	Front rungs	2 pcs.	$\frac{15}{16}$ x $17\frac{3}{4}$ *
E	Side and back seat rungs	2 pcs.	1 x $13\frac{1}{2}$ *
F	Side and back rungs	6 pcs.	$\frac{15}{16}$ x $13\frac{1}{2}$ *
G	Slats	2 pcs.	$\frac{1}{4}$ x 2 x $13\frac{1}{2}$ **

* Includes a $\frac{7}{8}$" tenon on each end.
** Includes a $\frac{3}{4}$" tenon on each end.

94

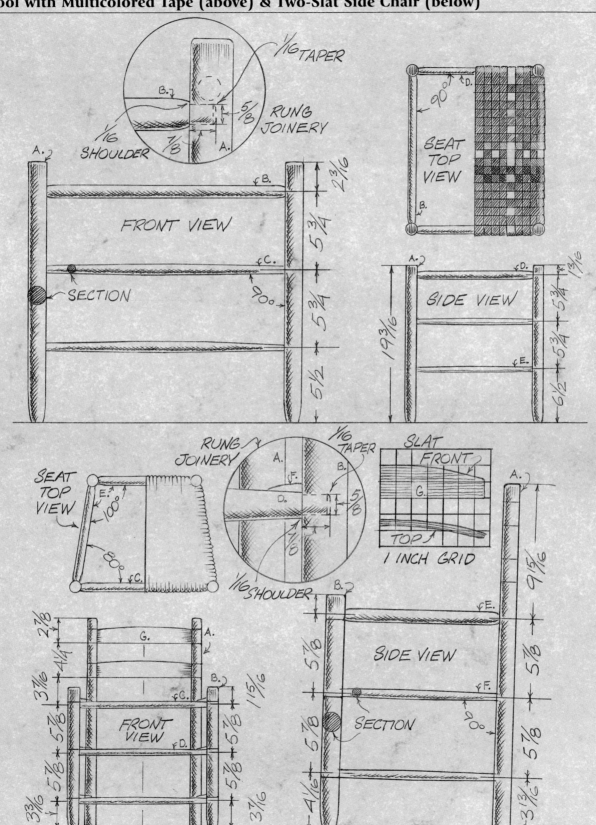

ENFIELD-STYLE SIDE CHAIR (cherry)

This chair is a variation of a mid-19th century one made at the Enfield, Connecticut, Shaker community. The slats, as on the original, are distinguished by a wide chamfer on their top, front edges. The main variation is the finial shape. To match a set of weaver's chairs already owned by my customer, the finial was changed from the original dainty shape to the more robust silhouette seen here.

The side rungs on most post-and-rung chairs enter the posts 90 degrees from the length of the post. However, because the Enfield chairs were produced without steam-bent back posts, the Shakers installed the side rungs approximately 2½ degrees off perpendicular. This gave the backs a relaxed stance, allowing the chair's occupant to lean back in a more comfortable posture.

This did spare them the labor of steam-bending the back parts, but it also added an extra complication to the drilling of the side rung mortises because not only were these mortises 97½ degrees from the back rungs and 82½ degrees from the front rungs, they also had to be angled 2½ degrees from the perpendicular in relation to the posts.

Although I was at first wary of the extra complexity, the result turned out to be relatively easy to achieve. The angles at which the side rungs meet both the back and front rungs were already established by the SRMJ. All I had to do was cock the drill press table 2½ degrees from perpendicular to introduce the tilting element. It did, nevertheless, require some careful work during the mortising process. A single chair required four different machine setups for the boring of the side rung mortises—two for the front ladder and two for the back ladder—and a single error in setup would have resulted in a blown chair.

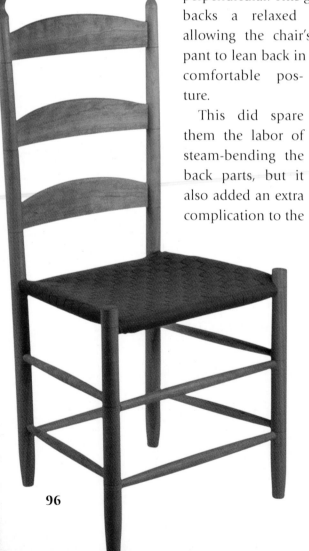

MATERIALS LIST

A	Back posts	2 pcs.	1⅜ dia. x 41⅛
B	Front side chair posts	2 pcs.	1⅜ dia. x 19⅛
C	Top slat	1 pc.	¼ x 3¹⁄₁₆ x 15¼ *
D	Middle slat	1 pc.	¼ x 3¹⁄₁₆ x 15 **
E	Bottom slat	1 pc.	¼ x 3¹⁄₁₆ x 14¾ **
F	Front seat rung	1 pc.	1⅛ dia. x 18⅝ ✤
G	Front rungs	2 pcs.	⅞ dia. x 18⅝ ✤
H	Side seat rungs	2 pcs.	1⅛ dia. x 14¼ ✤
I	Side and bottom back rungs	5 pcs.	⅞ x 14¼ ✤
J	Back seat rung	1 pc.	1⅛ x 14¾ ✤

* Includes a ⅝" tenon on each end.
** Includes a ¾" tenon on each end.
✤ Includes a ⅞" tenon on each end.

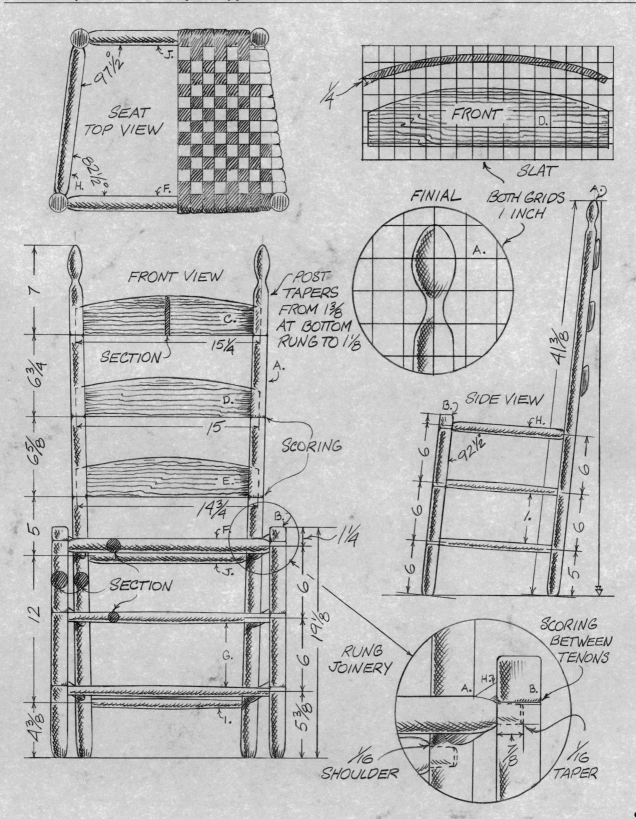

SEAT TOP VIEW

97½

82½°

J.

H.

F.

FRONT

SLAT

¼

D.

FINIAL

A.

BOTH GRIDS
1 INCH

FRONT VIEW

7

6¾

6⅝

5

12

4⅜

C.

SECTION

15¼

A.

D.

15

SCORING

E.

14¾

B.

F.

J.

SECTION

G.

I.

POST
TAPERS
FROM 1⅜
AT BOTTOM
RUNG TO 1⅛

1¼

6

19⅛

6

5⅜

RUNG
JOINERY

SIDE VIEW

B.

H.

92½°

4⅜

A.

6

6

6

6

6

6

6

5

1.

SCORING
BETWEEN
TENONS

A.

H.

B.

⅛

1/16
SHOULDER

1/16
TAPER

#5 SLAT-BACK SIDE CHAIR (cherry)

To meet the needs of their customers, the Shakers at the Mt. Lebanon factory offered their chairs in a variety of sizes, ranging from #0, the smallest, to #7, the largest. The smallest chairs on this numerical scale were suitable only for very young children, while those offered as #7's were comfortable only for the largest men of that era. Those chairs in the middle of the scale were sized to accommodate the bodies of the average men and women of that time.

Due, presumably, to better nutrition and better health care, the average person living in late-twentieth-century America is larger than the average person living in late-nineteenth-century America, the golden era of Shaker chair manufacturing. As a result, those chairs in the middle of the Shakers' size range—the #3's and the #4's—don't fit contemporary Americans quite so well. In fact, in my chair-making business, I rarely build a chair on the lower half of the Shakers' numerical scale. The most popular size I offer is the #5, which seems to be just about right for a contemporary American of average stature.

MATERIALS LIST

A	Front posts	2 pcs.	$1\frac{7}{16}$ x $19\frac{1}{4}$
B	Back posts	2 pcs.	$1\frac{7}{16}$ x $40\frac{7}{8}$
C	Front seat rung	1 pc.	1 x $19\frac{3}{4}$ *
D	Front rungs	2 pcs.	$\frac{15}{16}$ x $19\frac{3}{4}$ *
E	Side seat rungs	2 pcs.	1 x $16\frac{1}{2}$ *
F	Side rungs	4 pcs.	$\frac{7}{8}$ x $16\frac{1}{2}$ *
G	Back seat rung	1 pc.	1 x $15\frac{1}{2}$ *
H	Back rung	1 pc.	$\frac{7}{8}$ x $15\frac{1}{2}$ *
I	Bottom slat	1 pc.	$\frac{1}{4}$ x $2\frac{5}{8}$ x $15\frac{1}{2}$ **
J	Lower middle slat	1 pc.	$\frac{1}{4}$ x $2\frac{5}{8}$ x $15\frac{3}{4}$ **
K	Upper middle slat	1 pc.	$\frac{1}{4}$ x $2\frac{5}{8}$ x 16 ✢
L	Top slat	1 pc.	$\frac{1}{4}$ x $2\frac{5}{8}$ x 16 ✢✢

* Includes a $\frac{7}{8}$" tenon on each end.
** Includes a $\frac{3}{4}$" tenon on each end.
✢ Includes a $\frac{5}{8}$" tenon on each end.
✢✢ Includes a $\frac{1}{2}$" tenon on each end.

#5 TAPE-BACK SIDE CHAIR (cherry)

Assembly of this chair is the same as for the #5 slat-back side chair described on the opposite page.

MATERIALS LIST

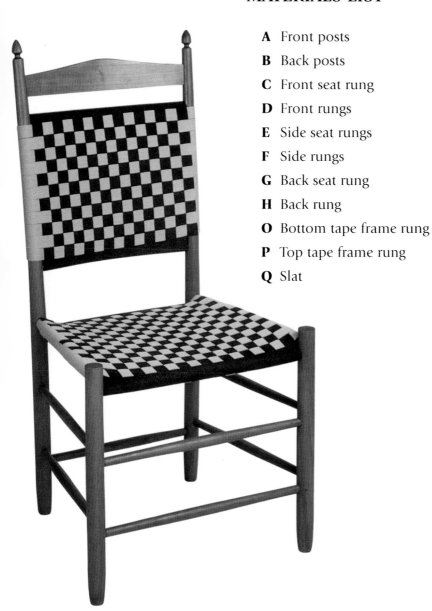

A	Front posts	2 pcs.	1$\frac{7}{16}$ x 19$\frac{1}{4}$
B	Back posts	2 pcs.	1$\frac{7}{16}$ x 40$\frac{7}{8}$
C	Front seat rung	1 pc.	1 x 19$\frac{3}{4}$ *
D	Front rungs	2 pcs.	$\frac{15}{16}$ x 19$\frac{3}{4}$ *
E	Side seat rungs	2 pcs.	1 x 16$\frac{1}{2}$ *
F	Side rungs	4 pcs.	$\frac{7}{8}$ x 16$\frac{1}{2}$ *
G	Back seat rung	1 pc.	1 x 15$\frac{1}{2}$ *
H	Back rung	1 pc.	$\frac{7}{8}$ x 15$\frac{1}{2}$ *
O	Bottom tape frame rung	1 pc.	$\frac{3}{4}$ x 16 **
P	Top tape frame rung	1 pc.	$\frac{3}{4}$ x 16$\frac{1}{2}$ ✤
Q	Slat	1 pc.	$\frac{1}{4}$ x 2$\frac{5}{8}$ x 16$\frac{1}{2}$ ✤

* Includes a $\frac{7}{8}$" tenon on each end.
** Includes a $\frac{5}{8}$" tenon on each end.
✤ Includes a $\frac{1}{2}$" tenon on each end.

#5 TAPE-BACK ARMCHAIR (cherry)

Except for the arms, mushroom caps, and front posts, the assembly of both of these armchairs is the same as for the #5 side chairs described on previous pages.

The extra pieces necessary for constructing these

#5 SLAT-BACK ARMCHAIR

armchairs are detailed in the Additional Materials List below and in the measured drawings on the opposite page.

Just as with the side chairs, the back can be finished with slats or with tape.

ADDITIONAL MATERIALS LIST (for armchairs)

A-1	Front posts	2 pcs.	$1\frac{7}{16}$ x $24\frac{7}{8}$
M	Arms	2 pcs.	$\frac{5}{8}$ x 3 x $17\frac{5}{8}$ *
N	Mushroom caps	2 pcs.	$\frac{9}{16}$ x $1\frac{5}{8}$

* Includes a $\frac{7}{8}$" tenon on one end.
Note: This tenon is only ½" in diameter.

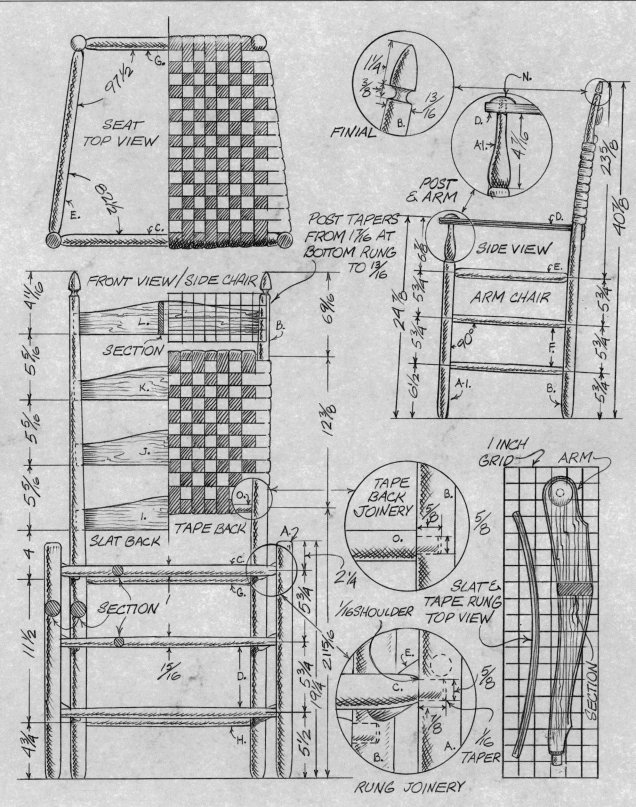

SEAT TOP VIEW

97½

82½

E.

C.

G.

FINIAL

1¼
3/8
13/16
B.

POST & ARM

N.

D.

A-1.

4 1/16

SIDE VIEW

ARM CHAIR

POST TAPERS FROM 1 7/16 AT BOTTOM RUNG TO 13/16

D.

E.

F.

90°

A-1.

B.

24 7/8
5¾
5¾
5¾
6½

23 5/8
40 7/8
5¾
5¾
5¾

FRONT VIEW / SIDE CHAIR

4¼
5½
5½
5½
5½
4

SECTION

L.

K.

J.

I.

SLAT BACK

TAPE BACK

B.

O.

6 9/16

12 7/8

TAPE BACK JOINERY

B.
5/8
5/8
O.

1 INCH GRID

ARM

SLAT & TAPE RUNG TOP VIEW

SECTION

SECTION

C.
G.
A-2

2¼

1/16 SHOULDER

5¾
5¾
2 15/16
19¼

D.

H.

15/16

11½

4¾

5½

RUNG JOINERY

E.
C.
B.
A.
1/8
1/16 TAPER
5/8

TAPE-BACK SETTEE (white ash)

My eight-year-old son, Andy, loves this chair. He leans a pillow against one of the arms and stretches out lengthwise, his head on the pillow, his body wrapped in a blanket, to watch television.

The settee is, however, a bit shallow, front-to-back, for an adult. Bending the back posts would add some depth, but the two settees that I have built since making this one have appreciably deeper seats, which puts the front seat rung in contact with the backs of the thighs at a more comfortable location.

MATERIALS LIST

A	Front posts	2 pcs.	$1\frac{7}{16}$ x $24\frac{7}{8}$
B	Back posts	2 pcs.	$1\frac{7}{16}$ x $40\frac{7}{8}$
C	Front seat rung	1 pc.	$1\frac{3}{8}$ x $37\frac{3}{4}$ *
D	Front rungs	2 pcs.	$1\frac{1}{4}$ x $37\frac{3}{4}$ *
E	Side seat rungs	2 pcs.	$1\frac{3}{8}$ x $16\frac{1}{2}$ *
F	Side rungs	4 pcs.	$1\frac{1}{8}$ x $16\frac{1}{2}$ *
G	Back seat rung	1 pc.	$1\frac{3}{8}$ x $33\frac{3}{8}$ *
H	Back rung	1 pc.	$1\frac{1}{4}$ x $33\frac{3}{8}$ *
I	Bottom tape frame rung	1 pc.	$1\frac{1}{8}$ x $33\frac{1}{2}$ **
J	Top tape frame rung	1 pc.	$1\frac{1}{8}$ x $34\frac{1}{4}$ **
K	False back posts	2 pcs.	$1\frac{1}{8}$ x $17\frac{5}{8}$ ✢
L	Arms	2 pcs.	$\frac{5}{8}$ x 3 x $17\frac{5}{8}$ ✢✢
M	Mushroom caps	2 pcs.	$\frac{9}{16}$ x $1\frac{5}{8}$

* Includes a $\frac{7}{8}$" tenons on each end.

** Includes a $\frac{5}{8}$" tenons on each end.

✢ Includes a $\frac{1}{2}$" tenons on each end.

✢✢ Includes a $\frac{7}{8}$" tenon on one end. Note: This tenon is only $\frac{1}{2}$" in diameter.

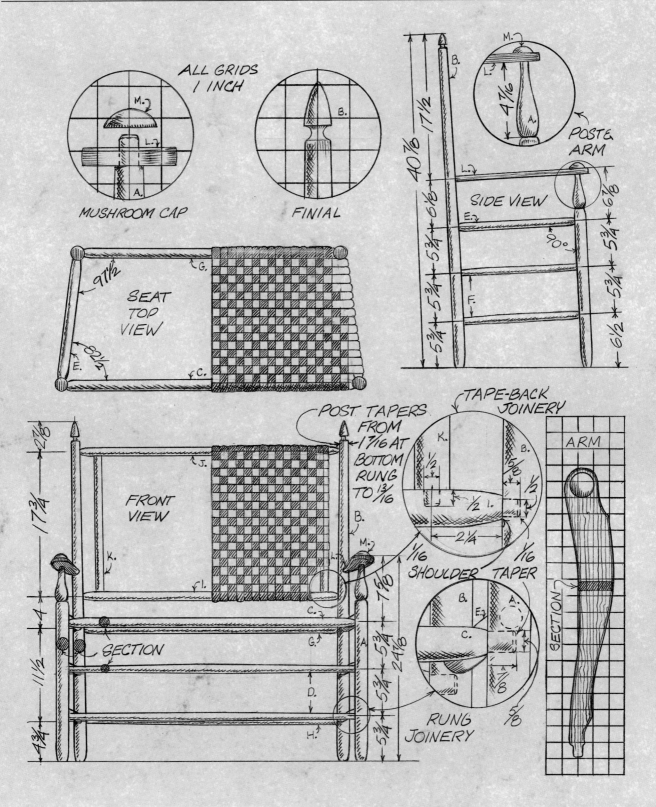

ALL GRIDS 1 INCH

MUSHROOM CAP

FINIAL

POST & ARM

SIDE VIEW

SEAT TOP VIEW

TAPE-BACK JOINERY

ARM

POST TAPERS FROM 1 7/16 AT BOTTOM RUNG TO 13/16

FRONT VIEW

SECTION

SHOULDER TAPER

RUNG JOINERY

MT. LEBANON SLAT-BACK TRANSITIONAL ROCKERS

▲ with Cushion Rail (walnut)

This chair, a measured drawing of which appears in John Kassay's *The Book of Shaker Furniture*, has been the foundation of my chair-making business. The first six or eight chairs sold were variations of this form, and it remains one of the most popular chairs I make.

The term *transitional*, in this context, indicates that this form is one typical of that period when Shaker chair-making was changing from shop-built to factory-built chairs.

MATERIALS LIST

A	Front posts	2 pcs.	1⅜ x 20½
B	Back posts	2 pcs.	1⅜ x 42⅞ *
C	Front seat rung	1 pc.	1 x 21¼ **
D	Front rungs	2 pcs.	⅞ x 21¼ **
E	Side seat rungs	2 pcs.	1 x 16½ **
F	Side rungs	4 pcs.	⅞ x 16½ **
G	Back seat rung	1 pc.	1 x 15½ **
H	Back rungs	2 pcs.	⅞ x 15½ **
I	Bottom slat	1 pc.	¼ x 2½ x 16 **
J	Lower middle slat	1 pc.	¼ x 2½ x 16¼ **
K	Upper middle slat	1 pc.	¼ x 2½ x 16½ **
L	Top slat	1 pc.	¼ x 2½ x 16¼ ♣
M	Cushion rail	1 pc.	¹¹⁄₁₆ x 19
N	Rockers	2 pcs.	⅜ x 3¾ x 28
O	Arms	2 pcs.	⅝ x 3 x 17⅝ ♣♣
P	Mushroom caps	2 pcs.	⁹⁄₁₆ x 1⅝
Q	Rocker pegs	4 pcs.	³⁄₁₆ x 1⅜ ♦

* Tenons at the top of the posts should be made 1/8" longer than is indicated by this finished post length so that they can be pared flush with the outside diameter of the cushion rail.

** Includes a ⅞" tenon on each end.

♣ Includes a ½" tenon on each end.

♣♣ Includes a ⅞" tenon on one end. Note: This tenon is only ½" in diameter.

♦ After fitting, these are pared flush with the outside diameter of this post.

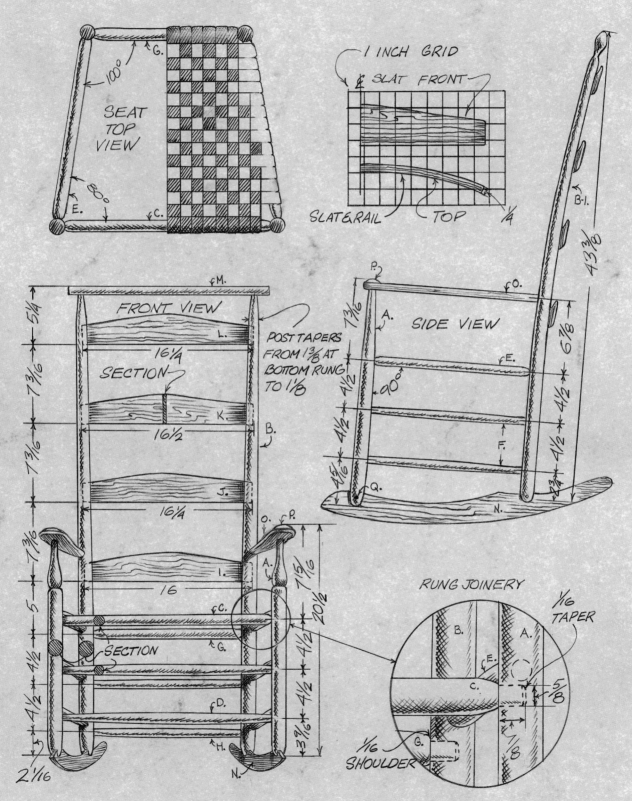

SEAT TOP VIEW

100°

80°

G.

E.

C.

1 INCH GRID

SLAT FRONT

SLAT&RAIL

TOP

1/4

B-1.

43 3/8

FRONT VIEW

M.

SECTION

SECTION

L.

K.

J.

I.

16 1/4

16 1/2

16 1/4

16

5 1/4

7 3/16

7 3/16

7 3/16

5

4 1/2

4 1/2

3

2 1/16

C.

G.

D.

H.

N.

B.

O.

P.

A.

POST TAPERS FROM 1 3/8 AT BOTTOM RUNG TO 1 1/8

SIDE VIEW

P.

O.

A.

E.

F.

Q.

N.

7 3/16

4 1/2

4 1/2

4 1/2

6 1/8

4 1/2

4 1/2

90°

7 9/16

20 1/2

4 1/2

3 9/16

RUNG JOINERY

1/16 TAPER

1/16 SHOULDER

A.

B.

C.

E.

G.

5/8

1/8

MT. LEBANON SLAT-BACK TRANSITIONAL ROCKERS

▲ with Bulbous Finials (cherry)

Assembly and the materials list are the same as for the Mt. Lebanon rocker presented on the previous two pages except for the back post measurements. The back post measurements of this particular rocker are as follows:

B-1   Back posts   2 pcs.   1⅜ x 43⅜

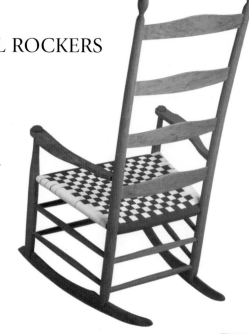

▲ with Sculpted Arms and Turned Vases (cherry)

Assembly and the materials list are the same as for the Mt. Lebanon transitional rockers above, except for the arm dimensions. The arm measurements of this particular rocker are as follows:

Notice also that this variation has a different shape below the cushion rail.

O-1   Arms   2 pcs.   1 x 3 x 17⅝

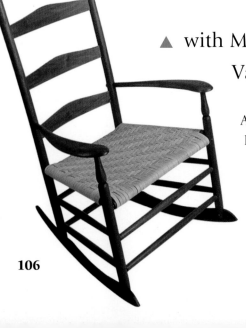

▲ with Mitten Arms and Turned
Vases (walnut)

Assembly and the materials list are the same as for the Mt. Lebanon transitional rockers above, except for the arm dimensions. The arm measurements of this particular rocker are as follows:

O-2   Arms   2 pcs.   ¾ x 3½ x 18

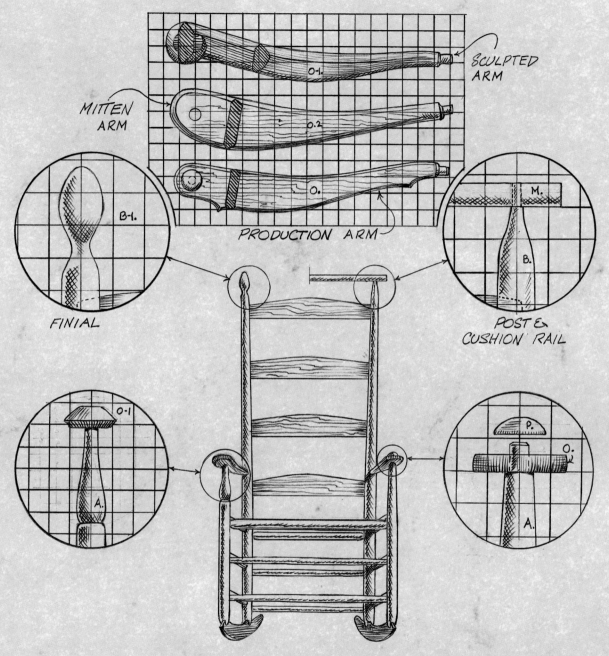

SCULPTED ARM

MITTEN ARM

O-1.

O-2.

O.

PRODUCTION ARM

B-1.

FINIAL

M.

B.

POST & CUSHION RAIL

O-1.

A.

P.

O.

A.

ALL GRIDS 1 INCH

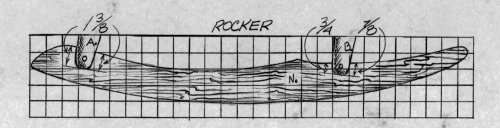

$1\frac{3}{8}$

A.

ROCKER

$\frac{3}{4}$

$\frac{1}{8}$

B.

N.

#7 SLAT-BACK ROCKER (curly maple and walnut)

The first four or five #7 rockers I built were sold, unseated, to a store in Cincinnati. The store owner then wove the tape before delivering the chairs to his customers. It wasn't until I built the curly maple and walnut slat-back shown on these pages that I had an opportunity to sit in one.

I really had no idea what I had been missing. Spacious and comfortable, this chair is eminently suitable for someone six feet tall or taller.

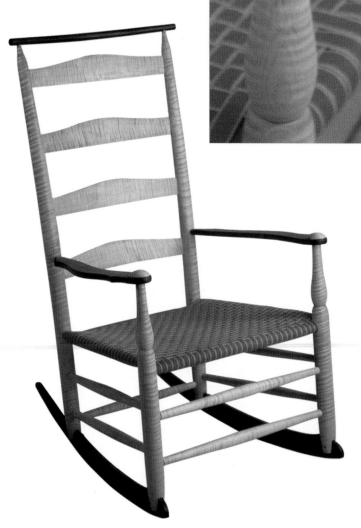

MATERIALS LIST

A	Front posts	2 pcs.	1¾ x 22¼
B	Back posts	2 pcs.	1¾ x 41 *
C	Front seat rung	1 pc.	1⅛ x 22 **
D	Front rungs	2 pcs.	1⅛ x 22 **
E	Side seat rungs	2 pcs.	1⅛ x 18½ **
F	Side rungs	4 pcs.	1⅛ x 18½ **
G	Back seat rung	1 pc.	1⅛ x 17¼ **
H	Back rung	1 pc.	1⅛ x 17¼ **
I	Bottom slat	1 pc.	⁹⁄₃₂ x 2¾ x 18 **
J	Lower middle slat	1 pc.	⁹⁄₃₂ x 2¾ x 18⅛ **
K	Upper middle slat	1 pc.	⁹⁄₃₂ x 2¾ x 18¼ **
L	Cushion rail	1 pc.	¾ x 20¾
M	Top slat	1 pc.	⁹⁄₃₂ x 2¾ x 18½ ✤
N	Arms	2 pcs.	¹¹⁄₁₆ x 3⅝ x 19⅝ ✤✤
O	Mushroom caps	2 pcs.	¹¹⁄₁₆ x 1⅞
P	Rockers	2 pcs.	⁷⁄₁₆ x ¾ x 30 ⅞
Q	Rocker pegs	4 pcs.	¹³⁄₁₆ x 1⅜

* Tenons at the top of the posts should be made ⅛" longer than is indicated by this finished post length so that they can be pared flush with the outside diameter of the cushion rail.

** Includes a ⅞" tenon on each end.

✤ Includes a ⅝" tenon on each end.

✤✤ Includes a ⅞" tenon on one end. Note: This tenon is ⅝" in diameter.

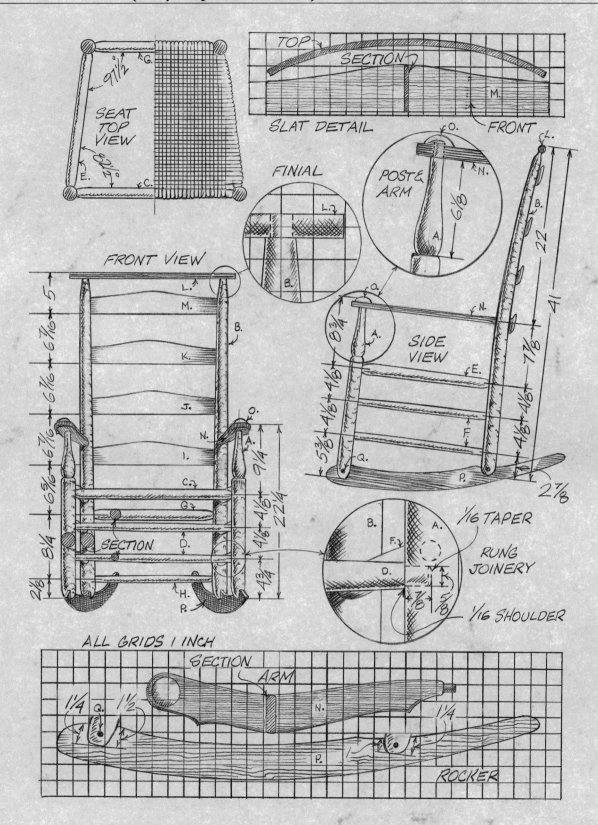

SEAT TOP VIEW

9½

G.

62½°

E.

C.

TOP

SECTION

SLAT DETAIL

M.

FRONT

FINIAL

L.

B.

POST & ARM

O.

N.

6⅛

A.

L.

B.

22

41

7⅞

FRONT VIEW

L.

M.

B.

K.

J.

O.

N.

A.

I.

C.

G.

SECTION

D.

H.

P.

5

6⅛

6⅛

6⅛

6⅛

6⅜

6¼

8¼

2⅜

7¼

4⅛

4½

22¼

4⅛

4¾

SIDE VIEW

O.

N.

A.

E.

F.

Q.

P.

8¼

5⅜

4⅛

4⅛

4⅛

4⅛

4¾

2⅞

B.

A.

1/16 TAPER

F.

RUNG JOINERY

D.

7/8

5/8

1/16 SHOULDER

ALL GRIDS 1 INCH

SECTION ARM

1¼

Q.

1½

N.

P.

1¼

ROCKER

#7 TAPE-BACK ROCKERS WITH SLAT (cherry)

▲ with Cushion Rail

Assembly of this #7 tape-back rocker with slat (and with cushion rail) is the same as for the #7 slat-back rocker presented on the previous two pages.

▲ without Cushion Rail

This chair differs from the one on the left of this page in only two respects: First, on this chair there is, of course, no cushion rail; second, on this chair the posts terminate in a delicate acorn finial.

MATERIALS LIST
(for both versions)

A	Front posts	2 pcs.	1⅜ x 22¼
B	Back posts	2 pcs.	1⅜ x 41 *
C	Front seat rung	1 pc.	1⅛ x 22 **
D	Front rungs	2 pcs.	1 x 22 **
E	Side seat rungs	2 pcs.	1⅛ x 18½ **
F	Side rungs	4 pcs.	15⁄16 x 18½ **
G	Back seat rung	1 pc.	1⅛ x 17¼ **
H	Back rung	1 pc.	15⁄16 x 17¼ **
I	Lower tape frame rung	1 pc.	¾ x 17¼ ✤

J	Upper tape frame rung	1 pc.	¾ x 18 ✤
K	Slat	1 pc.	¼ x 2⅝ x 18 ✤
L	Cushion rail	1 pc.	¾ x 20¾
M	Arms	2 pcs.	11⁄16 x 3⅝ x 19⅝ ✤✤
N	Mushroom caps	2 pcs.	11⁄16 x 1⅞
O	Rockers	2 pcs.	7⁄16 x 3¾ x 30⅞
P	Rocker pegs	4 pcs.	13⁄16 x 1⅜ ♦

* Tenons at the top of the posts should be made ⅛" longer than is indicated by this finished post length so that they can be pared flush with the outside diameter of the cushion rail.

** Includes a ⅞" tenon on each end.

✤ Includes a ⅝" tenon on each end.

✤✤ Includes a ⅞" tenon on one end.

♦ After fitting, these are pared flush with the outside diameters of the posts.

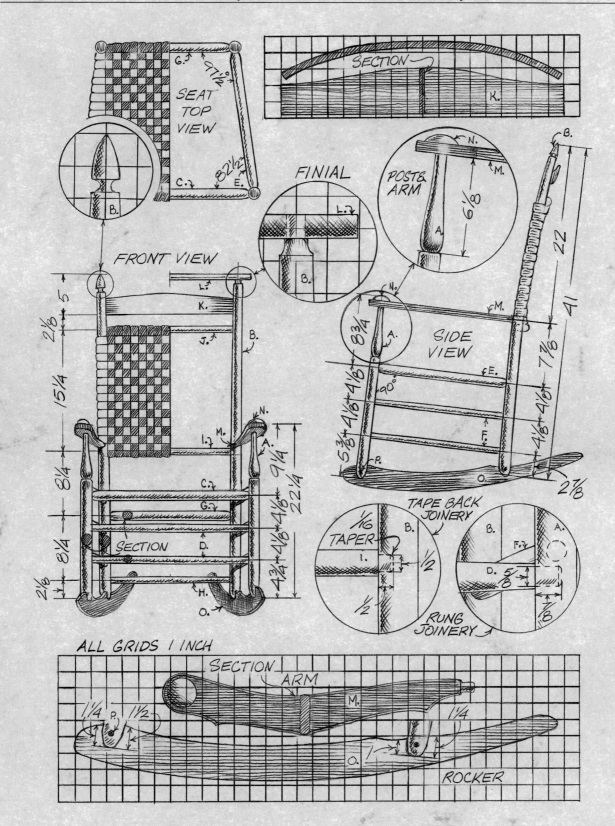

SEAT TOP VIEW

SECTION

FINIAL

POST & ARM

FRONT VIEW

SIDE VIEW

SECTION

TAPE BACK JOINERY

RUNG JOINERY

ALL GRIDS 1 INCH

SECTION ARM

ROCKER

Pilgrim Chairs

▲▽▲▽▲▽▲▽▲▽▲▽

Although I like the looks of the Pilgrim chairs on these four pages, I don't like the way they sit. The backs are straight, unrelieved by either steam-bent back posts or a woven back panel; and the turnings, so appealing to the eye, are much less appealing to the back. The Pilgrims must have been tough.

CARVER ARMCHAIR (cherry)

Less than fifty years after the Pilgrims landed in this country, these chairs—named for John Carver (1576–1621), who was the first governor of Plymouth Colony—were being made in sufficient numbers to have permitted many to survive until the twentieth century.

Although examples may differ in specific details, all are alike in several respects. First, all are post-and-rung chairs, the seat rungs of which provide a frame over which rush was woven (sometimes a leather seat was fastened over the seat rungs). Second, the chairs are all elaborately turned with a number of vases, coves, and beads adorning the lengths of the posts and the lengths of certain rungs as well as the vertical spindles. Third, between the back posts, above the seat, there is a rack of vertical turned spindles mortised into the rungs that connect the back posts.

The customer who ordered a pair of these chairs furnished me with a measured drawing, which I used less as a Bible than as a general reference. The rungs and spindles indicated by the drawing are a little heavier than those seen here, and the topmost ball on each finial is a little larger on my chair than those indicated by the drawing, although I can't now recall why I made the changes.

MATERIALS LIST

A	Back posts	2 pcs.	2 x 43
B	Front posts	2 pcs.	2 x 30½
C	Front seat rung	1 pc.	1⅛ x 21*
D	Front rungs	2 pcs.	1 x 21*
E	Back and side seat rungs	3 pcs.	1⅛ x 15*
F	Back and side rungs	11 pcs.	1 x 15*
G	Vertical spindles	3 pcs.	1 x 12**

* Includes a ⅞" tenon length on each end.
** Includes a ½" tenon length on each end.

Carver Armchair (cherry)

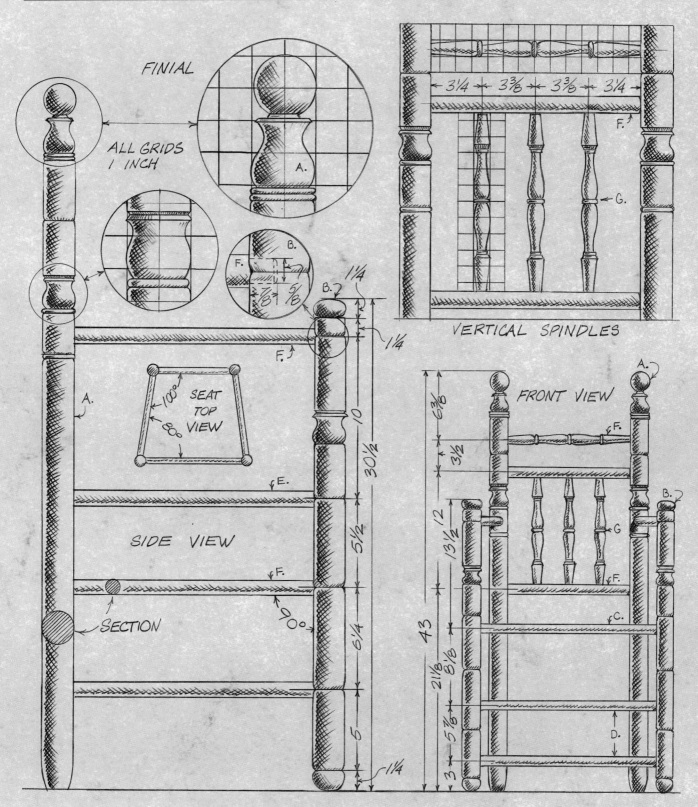

113

BREWSTER ARMCHAIR (cherry)

The same customer who ordered a pair of Carver chairs later ordered a pair of Brewster chairs. I agreed to take on the job even though, at the time, I could not recall ever having seen a photo of a Brewster chair.

Starting my preparations in the library, there, in addition to photos of a half dozen Brewster chairs, I found some gross measurements for this particular variety of Pilgrim furniture. Like the Carver chairs I'd already studied, these tended to be about 45" in height, with a front ladder width of about 23" and a back ladder width of about 17". The arms were lower than those on the Carver chair and the turning of the posts and the vertical spindles more elaborate. But the primary difference was the presence, on the Brewster chair, of a rack of vertical spindles on the front ladder below the seat and a double rack of vertical spindles on the back ladder above the seat.

I photocopied the pictures of Brewster chairs and began to establish some specific measurements.

Since the posts appeared to be heavier than those on the Carver chairs, I chose a diameter of 2¼". Post diameter wasn't indicated on any of the photos I'd photocopied, but the extra ¼" seemed about right. I decided that the back post length should be 43", the same as that on the Carver chairs; however, since the arms were lower on this new chair, I shortened the front posts to 26", again because this also seemed about right. Because of the similarity in chair width, I borrowed rung length measurements intact from the Carver chair.

Then, with the general values established, I pulled out a stack of layout sticks and began marking off the divisions for mortises and the various turned parts.

This is the chair that resulted from that preparation. While not an accurate reproduction of any specific original, any connoisseur of Pilgrim furniture would, I believe, instantly recognize this as a Brewster chair.

The Brewster has a number of elaborately turned parts.

MATERIALS LIST

A	Back posts	2 pcs.	2¼ x 43
B	Front posts	2 pcs.	2¼ x 26
C	Front seat rung	1 pc.	1⅛ x 21*
D	Front rungs	2 pcs.	1 x 21*
E	Back and side seat rungs	3 pcs.	1⅛ x 15*
F	Back and side rungs	11 pcs.	1 x 15*
G	Vertical spindles	9 pcs.	1⅛ x 7½**

* Includes a ⅞" tenon length on each end.
** Includes a ½" tenon length on each end.

114

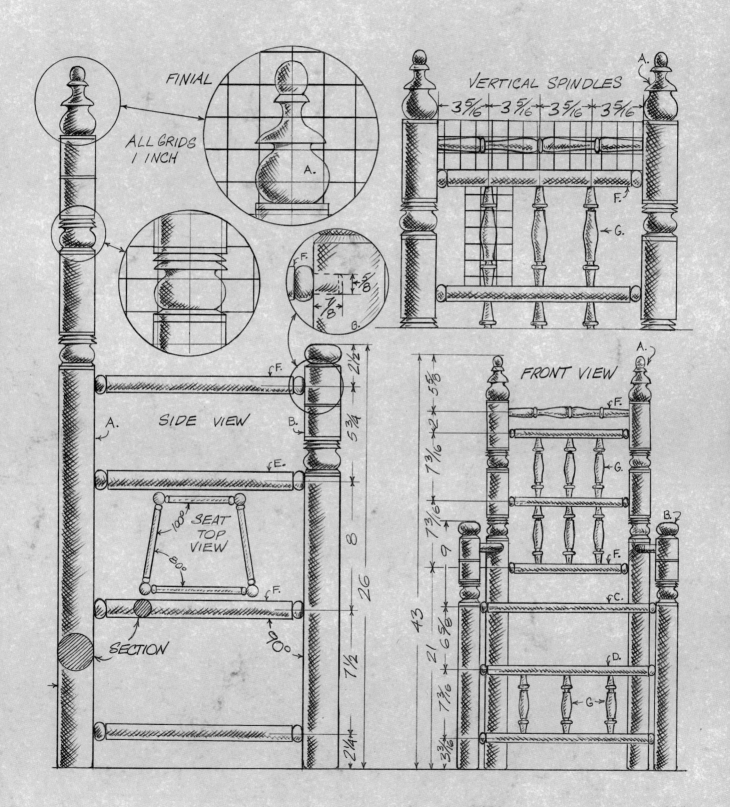

FINIAL

ALL GRIDS 1 INCH

A.

F.

B.

VERTICAL SPINDLES

3 5/16 — 3 5/16 — 3 5/16 — 3 5/16

A.

F.

G.

5/8

1/8

F.

A.

SIDE VIEW

B.

E.

SEAT TOP VIEW

100°

80°

F.

90°

SECTION

2 1/2

5 3/4

8

26

7 1/2

2 1/4

FRONT VIEW

A.

A.

F.

G.

F.

B.

C.

D.

G.

5 5/8

2

7 3/16

7 3/16

9

43

21

6 5/8

7 7/16

3 3/16

Contemporary
Post-and-Rung Chairs

▲▽▲▽▲▽▲▽▲▽▲▽▲▽

My first post-and-rung chairs were reproductions of Shaker originals. Like many woodworkers, I was drawn to their spry elegance, their sophistication, their spare and clean lines. Also like many woodworkers, I found those lines easier to reproduce than the convoluted shapes on, for instance, Brewster or Carver chairs.

Then gradually, over a period of years, I began tinkering with the plain and simple features of the Shaker chairs I built. Although still appreciating the honest simplicity of the originals, occasionally as I stood in my shop studying a recently completed chair, I found myself craving a bit more in the way of ornamentation.

I started with the arms—band-sawing new contours, sculpting with a drawknife and spokeshave, incising curlicues with a shop knife—in the process creating a number of shapes that could be substituted for the cookie-cutter arms on the Shaker originals.

Furthermore, I experimented with the slats. Some of mine, like the Shaker originals, were very simple in silhouette. Others expanded into more flamboyant shapes that the Shaker designers might have found unsettling. I tinkered with the Shaker finials, too. Although I didn't introduce any new shapes—it's hard to imagine any new lathe-turned forms—I did manipulate those on the Shaker originals, elongating some, compressing others, and joining shapes in ways not quite like those on the original chairs.

At first, my customers were hesitant to consider anything different from the examples pictured in books. But eventually that changed. Today some request the modified Shaker chairs. And still others request chairs that are unlike any Shaker or period originals—chairs of my own design.

BUBBLE-SLAT ROCKER (cherry) & SETTEE (walnut)

Early in the nineteenth century, Shaker chair-makers, like those in the outside world, built their chairs either one at a time or in small sets. But by the 1870s, Shaker

chairs were being mass-produced in the Mt. Lebanon operation, then marketed to the outside world. Chairs built in the early stages of mass production were sometimes referred to as "transitional" chairs because, although they may have been built with some of the features of earlier, hand-crafted chairs, they were, nonetheless, being produced in large numbers.

The very first Shaker chair I made was a transitional rocker—one illustrated in John Kassay's *The Book of Shaker Furniture*. The bubble-slat rocker shown here and the double rocker that follows at the end of this section are both based on the body of that transitional rocker.

First, I widened the original chair enough to accommodate the enclosed tape frame on the chair back without crowding the sitter's back between the two false back posts. Then, instead of bending the chair's outside back posts to create a comfortable seating angle between seat and back, I relied on the flexibility of the woven back panel to provide that comfort. Thus it was possible to leave the posts straight.

There are also a number of cosmetic changes that, combined, give this chair a non-Shaker look. The most obvious of these is the slat profile. It's wider than the slat on any Shaker chair and has a busier look. The bubble shapes of that profile are echoed in the round ball atop the finial and in the bubble turnings below the arms. Also, the arms are wider and more sculptural than any found on Shaker originals. The extra width provides elbow comfort, and the sculpture adds visual and tactile appeal.

117

MATERIALS LISTS

BUBBLE-SLAT ROCKER
(measured drawings on pages 121 & 123)

A	Front posts	2 pcs.	1⅜ x 20¾ *
B	Back posts	2 pcs.	1⅜ x 43½
C	Arms	2 pcs.	1 x 4¼ x 18¼ **
D	Back slat	1 pc.	¼ x 4¾ x 17¼ ✤
E	Rockers	2 pcs.	⅜ x 4 x 28
F	Front rungs	2 pcs.	⅞ x 23 ✤✤
G	Front seat rung	1 pc.	1⅛ x 23 ✤✤
H	Side rungs	4 pcs.	⅞ x 16½ ✤✤
I	Side seat rungs	2 pcs.	1⅛ x 16½ ✤✤
J	Back rungs	2 pcs.	⅞ x 17¼ ✤
K	Back seat and tape frame rungs	3 pcs.	1⅛ x 17¼ ✤✤
L	False back posts	2 pcs.	1⅛ x 19¼ ◆
M	Wedges	2 pcs.	⅛ x ⅝ x ¾
N	Rocker pegs	4 pcs.	3⁄16 x 1⅜ ◆◆

BUBBLE-SLAT SETTEE
(measured drawings opposite)

A	Back posts	2 pcs.	2⅛ x 45⅞
B	Front posts	2 pcs.	2⅛ x 25⅞ *
C	Arms	2 pcs.	15⁄16 x 4⅜ x 20⅝ **
D	Front seat rung	1 pc.	1⅜ x 38⅜ ✤
E	Front rungs	2 pcs.	15⁄16 x 38⅜ ✤
F	Side seat rungs	2 pcs.	1¼ x 18½ ✤
G	Side rungs	4 pcs.	1⅛ x 18½ ✤
H	Back seat rung	1 pc.	1⅜ x 33¼ ✤
I	Back rung	1 pc.	15⁄16 x 33¼ ✤
J	Bottom tape frame rung	1 pc.	15⁄16 x 33¼ ✤
K	Top tape frame rung	1 pc.	15⁄16 x 33½ ✤
L	False back posts	2 pcs.	15⁄16 x 17⅝ ✤✤
M	Slat	1 pc.	½ x 6½ x 33½ **
N	Wedges	2 pcs.	3⁄16 x ⅝ x ¾

* Tenons should be made ⅛" longer than is indicated by this finished post length so that they can be pared flush with top of arm after assembly.

** Includes a ⅞" tenon at end of arm. Note: This tenon is only ½" in diameter.

✤ Includes a ¾" tenon on each end.

✤✤ Includes a ⅞" tenon on each end.

◆ Includes a ½" tenon on each end.

◆◆ Rocker pegs are pared flush with the outside diameter of posts after assembly.

*Tenon should be made ⅛" longer than is indicated by this finished post length so that it can be pared flush with the top surface of the arm after assembly.

** Includes a ⅞" tenon on end. Note: Unlike the other tenons on this chair, this one is only ⅝" in diameter.

✤ Includes a ⅞" tenon on each end. Unlike most of the other tenons described in this book, these have a diameter of ¾".

✤✤ Includes a ½" tenon on each end.

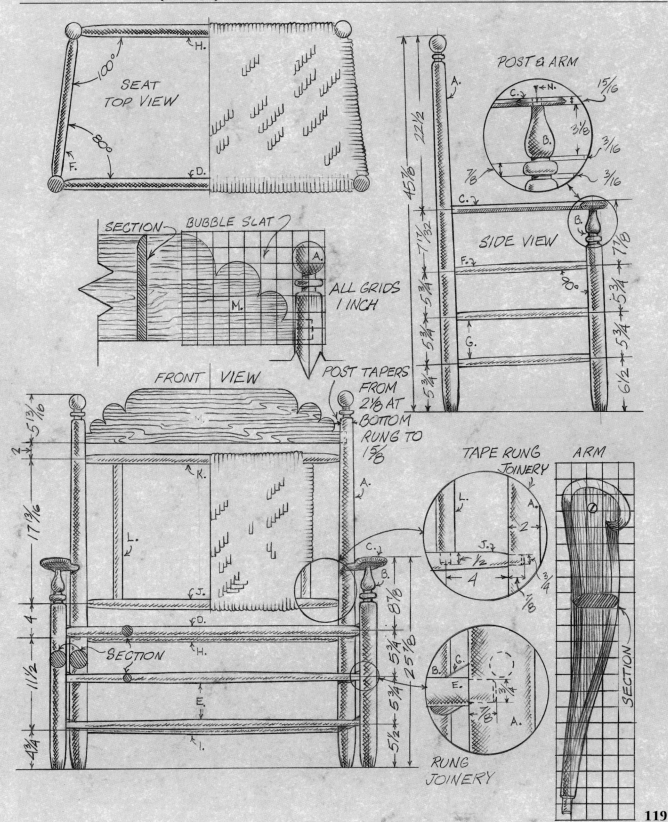

SEAT TOP VIEW

100°

80°

SECTION

BUBBLE SLAT

ALL GRIDS 1 INCH

POST TAPERS FROM 2⅛ AT BOTTOM RUNG TO 1⅝

FRONT VIEW

SECTION

POST & ARM

SIDE VIEW

TAPE RUNG JOINERY

RUNG JOINERY

ARM

SECTION

BLACK SHOES WITH TAPE/SPLINT BACK (cherry and walnut)

I began these chairs with a couple of exclamation marks, one on top of each of the back posts. I then added, below each arm, a variation of a vase I'd seen and admired on a number of chairs made at the Canterbury, New Hampshire, Shaker community. Because the exclamation marks and the vases were very different shapes, I put a pair of scored lines on the exclamation marks and a second pair of scored lines below the vase on each of the front posts to bring the chair's front and back posts together visually.

I assembled the chair, applied the finish and tucked it away in a corner of my storage room while working on a couple of sets of Shaker dining chairs. Then, several weeks later, I brought the chair out and prepared to weave the seat and back. Studying it while sipping a cup of coffee, I began to wonder what would happen if I brought that curlicue on the top face of each arm into a tighter spiral, one extending all the way to the through tenon at the top of the front post.

Then, even though the chair had received its full quota of three coats of finish, I got out a shop knife and a paring chisel and began to tinker with the curlicue. Stepping back later to study the effect of the change, I began to look at the rest of the chair.

I liked the turnings, I liked the scored lines, but not the slat. It was too plain. I began to wonder what it would look like if a pair of curlicues were incised on the slat, curlicues similar to the ones just put on the arms.

I got out my tools and went to work, once again cutting through the three coats of finish into the wood below. This time when I stepped back to look, I liked what I saw.

MATERIALS LIST

Assembly and the materials list are the same as for the Bubble-Slat Rocker (page 118) except for the back posts and back slat:

B-1 Back posts   2 pcs.   1⅜ x 44¼
D-1 Back slat   1 pc.   ¼ x 3 x 17¼*

* Includes a ¾" tenon on each end.

In an attempt to bring all the parts of the chair together visually, the shape of the incised slat curlicue as well as the pair of scored lines on the pommel are repeated elsewhere on the chair.

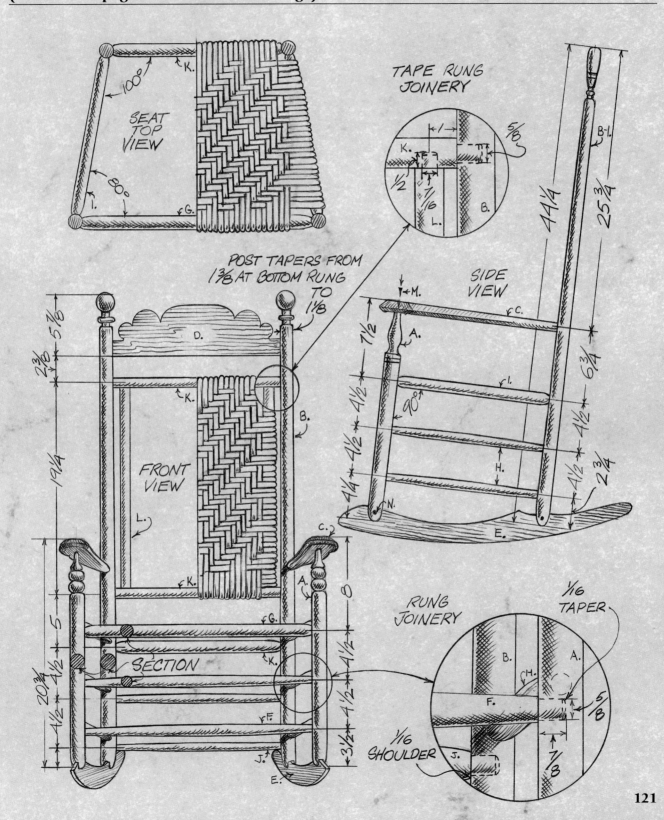

SEAT TOP VIEW

100°

80°

K.

I.

G.

TAPE RUNG JOINERY

5/8

K.

1/2

1/16

L.

B.

B-1.

44¼

25¾

SIDE VIEW

M.

A.

C.

7½

90°

I.

H.

6¾

4½

4½

4¼

4½

2¾

N.

E.

POST TAPERS FROM 1⅜ AT BOTTOM RUNG TO 1⅛

5⅛

2⅜

19¼

D.

K.

B.

FRONT VIEW

L.

C.

A.

O.

G.

K.

SECTION

F.

J.

E.

5

4½

20¾

4½

4½

4½

4½

3½

RUNG JOINERY

1/16 TAPER

B.

A.

H.

F.

5/8

J.

7/8

1/16 SHOULDER

CHAIR ARM (shaping) ▲▽▲▽▲▽▲▽▲▽▲▽▲▽▲▽▲▽▲▽▲▽▲▽▲▽▲▽▲▽▲▽▲

(Top) All the chairs I've designed have arms shaped by shaving and carving tools. Although the specific arm shapes may vary from chair to chair, the shaping technique remains the same.

After band-sawing the arm blank, I placed freehand lines on the top, bottom, and edges of those blanks to guide me in the shaping process. These arms had broad flat areas on their upper and lower surfaces. The borders of those flats were given crowned bevels, the limits of which are indicated by the pencil lines on the blank at the bottom of the picture.

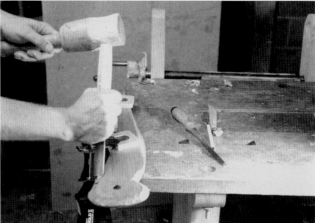

(Above middle) The bevel on the arm's end grain can be cut with the drawknife, but when working with dry stock, I find it easier to rough it in with a wide-sweep carving gouge.

The particular chip that was removed in this photo had to be cut free by twisting the gouge in a clockwise motion as it was driven into the work. Otherwise, a large section of the arm blank would have been split off due to the grain runout on that portion of the arm blank.

(Below middle) A drawknife was used to shape one of the bevels on the underside of the arm blank. Notice the wooden puppets that supported the work. These were mounted on a pipe clamp mounted in my vise. The tenon on one end of the arm blank was held in a ¾" hole in one puppet, while the other end was held in a depression that was dished into the face of the other puppet.

(Bottom) A spokeshave was used to give the bevels a smooth finish.

122

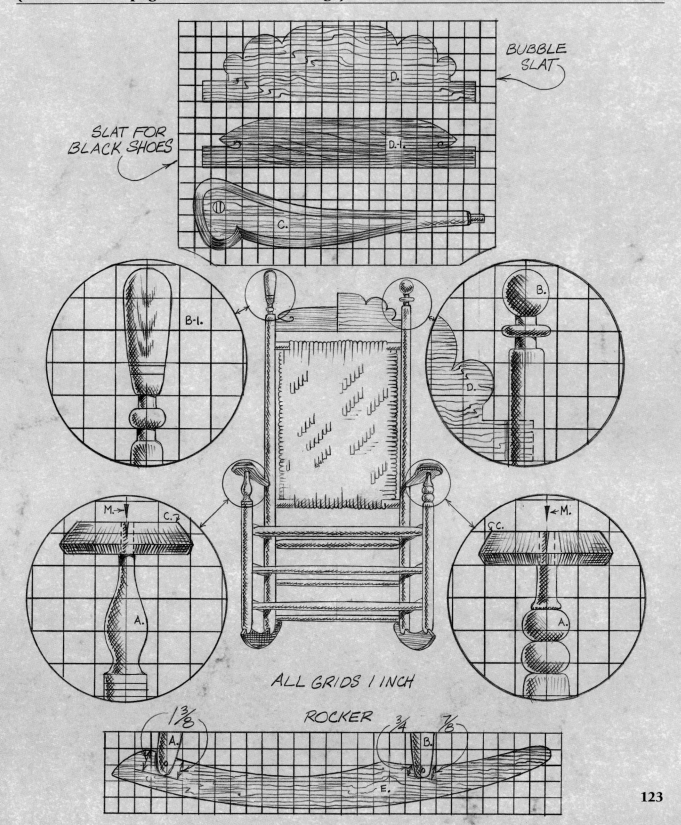

BUBBLE SLAT

SLAT FOR BLACK SHOES

ALL GRIDS 1 INCH

ROCKER

DOUBLE ROCKER (cherry)

I've always liked the idea of a double rocker, but haven't yet made one that is completely satisfactory, although some days, when I look at this one it seems to be reasonably close.

MATERIALS LIST

A	Back posts	2 pcs.	2⅛ x 43¼
B	Front posts	2 pcs.	2⅛ x 22³⁄₁₆ *
C	Front seat rung	1 pc.	1⅜ x 40 **
D	Front rungs	2 pcs.	1¼ x 40 **
E	Side seat rungs	2 pcs.	1⅜ x 18½ **
F	Side rungs	4 pcs.	1³⁄₁₆ x 18½ **
G	Back seat rung	1 pc.	1⅜ x 35¼ **
H	Back rung	1 pc.	1¼ x 35¼ **
I	top frame rung	1 pc.	1¼ x 35¾ **
J	Bottom tape frame rung	1 pc.	1¼ x 35¼ **
K	False back post	1 pc.	1¼ x 16⅛ ✣
L	Arms	2 pcs.	⅞ x 5 x 21¼ ✣✣
M	Rockers	2 pcs.	⅝ x 3¾ x 30¾
N	Slat	1 pc.	½ x 5 x 35¾ ♦
O	Rocker pegs	4 pcs.	³⁄₁₆ x 2¼ ♦♦
P	Wedges	2 pcs.	⅛ x ¾ x ¾

* Tenons should be made ⅛" longer than is indicated by this finished post length so that they can be pared flush with the top surface of the arm after assembly.

** Includes a ⅞" tenon on each end. Unlike most of the other rung tenons described in this book, these have a diameter of ¾".

✣ Includes a ½ x ½ tenon on each end.

✣✣ Includes a ⅞" tenon on one end. Unlike the others on this chair, this tenon is only ⅝" in diameter.

♦ Includes a ¾" tenon on each end.

♦♦ After fitting, these are pared flush with the outside diameter of the post.

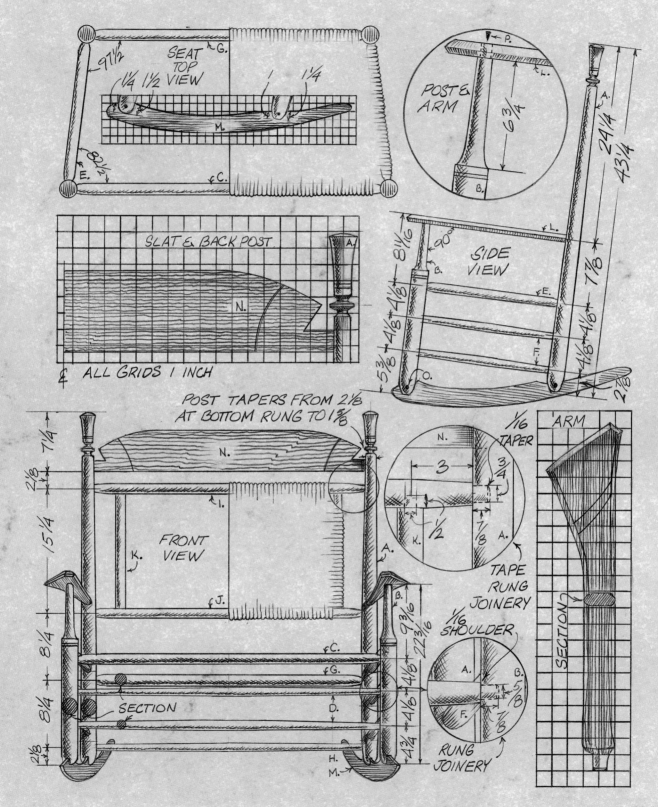

SEAT TOP VIEW

9 1/2

1 1/4   1 1/2

82 1/2

E.

G.

M.

C.

1   1 1/4

POST & ARM

6 3/4

P.

L.

B.

24 1/4

43 1/4

7 7/8

A.

SLAT & BACK POST

A.

N.

ALL GRIDS 1 INCH

SIDE VIEW

90°

B.

8 1/4

5 5/8   4 1/8   4 1/8

E.

F.

O.

2 1/8

4 1/8   4 1/8

POST TAPERS FROM 2 1/8
AT BOTTOM RUNG TO 1 5/8

FRONT VIEW

N.

I.

J.

C.

G.

D.

SECTION

7 1/4

2 1/8

15 1/4

8 1/4

8 1/4

2 1/8

H.

M.

B.

9 3/16

22 3/16

4 3/4   4 1/8   4 1/8

N.

3

3/4

1/2

7/8

A.

K.

1/16 TAPER

TAPE RUNG JOINERY

1/16 SHOULDER

A.

B.

F.

5/8

1 1/8

RUNG JOINERY

ARM

SECTION

125

Swings

▲▽▲▽▲▽▲▽▲▽▲▽

When I was a boy, I had a rope swing on a walnut tree that stood on the edge of our back garden, and many nights my friends and I swung there, hour after hour, higher and higher.

No one was hurt and no one was sued. But today, lawyers rule the world.

When I visited a local supplier of building materials to choose the rope for the one-board swing, I was surprised to see that not one single rope was approved for the support of human weight. In fact, each coil that I examined had a sticker indicating it was specifically <u>not</u> designed to support human weight. This was true for ropes woven of natural fibers and for ropes woven of synthetic fibers. This was true for ropes with a listed working weight of 50 pounds and for ropes with a listed working weight of 400 pounds.

I understand the manufacturer's caution. But it's still troubling.

ONE-BOARD SWING (white ash)

In the interests of safety, I did make a few changes from the swing I'd had when I was a boy.

First, I wrapped the cut ends with black electrician's tape to prevent fraying. Second, I rounded the sharp edges of the hole in the seat through which the rope passes, to remove the sharp wooden edge. I also wrapped tape around that part of the rope that passed through the hole. And third, where the rope passes over the limb of our ash tree, it is held in place by a couple of nails clenched across it. These nails prevent the rope from rubbing against the rough bark when the swing is being used.

MATERIALS LIST

A	Seat	1 pc.	1⅛ x 8⅛ x 19¼
B	Rope	1 pc.	¾ x amount needed
C	Tape	3 pcs	as needed
D	Boy or Girl	1 pc.	8 x 14 x 49½

And last, I told my son that at the end of the warm, summer season, we'll cut the rope down and throw it out. Next year, we'll have a new rope.

PORCH SWING (white ash)

This swing is big enough for two, and because of its sturdy ash frame, it's strong enough for more than two.

The seat panel is attached to the back at an angle of 97½ degrees; however, the mortises for the side seat rung tenons and for the arm tenons can't be drilled on the SRMJ because the jig's fence gets in the way.

To cut these mortises, I first installed the FRMJ on my drill press table. Then I set its fence ¹³⁄₁₆" from the lead point of the Forstner bit (¹³⁄₁₆" is half the diameter of the swing's posts). After assembling the back frame, I taped a two-foot level to one of the long, back rungs. Then, resting one end of the back panel on the FRMJ so that the post was crowded against the fence, I moved the other end of the back frame up and down until the level indicated that the long rungs were perpendicular to the axis of the Forstner bit. I then brought the bit into the post, cutting the mortises for the side seat rung tenons and for the arm tenons.

The lengths of nylon chair webbing were fastened into place with drywall screws passing through finishing washers. The finishing washers pressing against the doubled-up webbing at the end of each strip provided a larger bearing surface than would the screwheads alone. I used two screws at each end of the long seat strips and one screw at each end of all the other strips.

MATERIALS LIST

A	Long seat and back rungs	4 pcs.	1⅝ x 44¼ *
B	Side seat rungs	2 pcs.	1⅝ x 19 **
C	Side back rungs	2 pcs.	1⅝ x 28⅝
D	Arms	2 pcs.	1⅝ x 14½
E	Arm supports	2 pcs.	1⅝ x 10¼ *
F	Nylon chair webbing		120 ft.
G	Eye bolts and nuts	4 pcs.	¼ x 4
H	Drywall screws		
I	Finishing washers		

* Includes 1" tenon on each end. Unlike most of the rung tenons in this book, all the tenons on this swing have a diameter of ¾".

** Includes 1" tenon on one end.

Porch Swing (white ash)

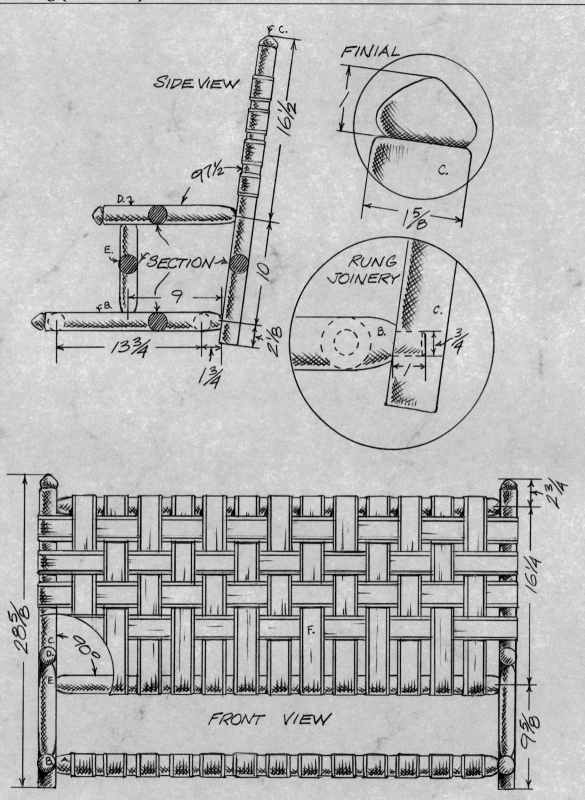

SIDE VIEW

FINIAL

SECTION

RUNG JOINERY

FRONT VIEW

RUNNING A SMALL SHOP

In a production woodworking shop, an individual craftsman is likely to perform the same narrowly defined task over and over again. There are advantages to such a practice. It does allow the craftsman to develop extraordinary skill, which translates into increased speed and productivity, which means greater shop profit. However, repetition can also lead to other, less desirable results.

Eight hours at the same machine, performing the same task, can leave the craftsman bored; and as the mind wanders, so do the eyes and hands. The hazards implicit in production work cannot be overstated.

The psychological effects of boredom are nearly as important. As much as possible, we should enjoy the experience of working, taking from it not only the money needed for the care and feeding of families, homes, cars, but also generous helpings of pleasure and satisfaction. After a week at the lathe turning chair rungs, the woodworker may wonder if his profession is any less drudging than traditional factory work.

However, with careful planning a craftsman in a small-shop can enjoy some of the advantages of production work without experiencing all of its miseries. What is needed is a workable compromise between speed and pleasure. By almost any standards, my shop is small, consisting of two rooms: a wood storage room that includes my thickness planer; and a workroom.

The workroom measures 10 by 24 feet, and it contains not only a workbench and my collection of hand tools but also all of my stationary power equipment: a table saw, a jointer, a radial-arm saw (with generous infeed and outfeed tables that double as extra workbenches), a lathe, a band saw, a drill press and, most important in December, a big wood burning stove around which I keep a couple of feet of empty air to minimize the possibility of an accidental fire.

MANAGEMENT

The shop is a cramped but functional working environment, and over the last ten years I've gotten fairly comfortable with its limitations. By the time Mark Prince, the owner of The Shaker Seedbox Company in Cincinnati, called to ask about the set of eight dining chairs pictured here, I had accumulated a fair amount of experience moving groups of chairs through my tiny shop. Most of the chairs I build are sold in sets—two, four, six—and even when I'm not building a set, it isn't unusual to have four or five individual chairs in varying states of completion scattered around the workroom. But this was my first opportunity to build eight chairs for a single buyer, as well as my first opportunity to build an entire set from figured wood.

Materials

When pricing a job, material is always the first consideration. This is especially true when the material is figured wood, which is always expensive and not always available in the required dimensions and quantities. After Mark and I had determined the exact characteristics of the chairs he wanted built, I got on the phone and attempted to track down the lumber.

Although many of my Shaker reproduction and Shaker-style chairs are made from a variety of woods including cherry, walnut, ash, and oak, most are constructed of hard maple, the material most used by the Shakers for chair-making. Hard maple is a good choice for this application since it combines enormous strength with a dense grain that holds turned detail very nicely.

My first problem was finding hard curly maple in the thickness required for post stock: a minimum of ⁶/₄. After the first few calls to dealers who specialized in figured wood, I found that while soft curly maple was relatively common in ⁶/₄ and ⁸/₄ thicknesses, hard curly maple (fiddleback) was extremely rare.

Making this search even more difficult was the fact that I wanted green post stock so that the post mortises could be allowed to shrink down on the dry rung tenons. A couple of the dealers I spoke with laughed when they learned what I wanted. It wasn't long before I was laughing with them.

After two weeks and countless phone calls, I spoke with Mark and told him that I couldn't do the job because the material simply didn't exist. Having already sold a customer on the considerable price of the chairs, he was reluctant to give it up. We discussed the possibilities, even briefly considering kiln-dried hard maple for post stock. Then, I had one more idea.

Not all soft maples share the same physical characteristics. The silver maple that grew in my region of the Untied States was much too soft for chair construction—something I had tested several years earlier. But there were other maples classified as soft that I thought might have the strength needed.

Calling the USDA Forest Products Lab in Wisconsin, one of their scientists explained that while hard maple is stronger than any of the soft maples, the red soft maple produced a wood that outperformed cherry in tests of strength. It was his opinion that red soft maple would produce satisfactory chair posts.

Encouraged by this conversation, I called Mark to discuss the possibilities. Having made a large number of chairs in cherry without a single part failure, I felt confident about building a chair from an even stronger wood. The only difficulty was estimating the effect curly figure might have on the strength of the chair posts. Curly figure makes parts more susceptible to fracture across the grain; and no one—not the Forest Products Lab or the National Hardwood Lumber Association—had test information on the strength of red maple exhibiting a curly figure. We decided to go ahead with it with one proviso: If, after I had assembled a test chair, there was evidence of weakness, we would turn the customer down.

The next step was estimating the amount of material the job would require. At $5.75 per board foot for ⁴/₄ curly maple rung stock, $6.20 per board foot for ¹²/₄ curly maple from which I would rip out post turning blanks, and $7.50 per board foot for the bird's-eye I would use for slats and arms, I didn't want to order too much, but also knew I wanted enough to be able to pick through the material in order to avoid making parts from stock with marginal figure.

A cabinetmaker estimates the amount of material the job requires, then adds 30 percent or 40 percent to account for defects and cut-offs. In post-and-rung chair-making, the rules are a little different. Everything depends on the stock from which the back posts are turned. While rungs and front posts can be made from the rips and cut-offs left behind after sizing back post stock, there must be a generous surplus of back post stock from which to choose. A single pea-sized knot along the length of a post sends it into the scrap bin—and I was ordering blind, over the phone.

For probably the fifth time, I called the only source I could find for green material, in Pennsylvania, this time asking about the length of the ¹²⁄₄ from which I would rip out my post stock. It measured 60 inches, close to ideal for back post stock, as it left me with enough length so that I could take some from either end of my 44" post stock to cut off any drying checks I might find.

I decided to order 60 board feet, almost five times what I would actually use in the back posts. That gave me the freedom to pick and choose my stock, with a little leeway in case I had to turn extra parts. The front post stock could be taken from the material rejected for back post use, since it's much easier to work around knots or stains when you're looking for a 20" length than it is when you're looking for a 44" length.

I added 22 board feet of ⁴⁄₄ curly maple for the rungs and 12 board feet of ⁴⁄₄ bird's-eye from which I would take the slats and arms. I ordered much more bird's-eye than I needed because its figure tends to run in streaks, and I wanted enough so that I could choose the areas of heaviest patterning for my slats and arms.

The seat rungs would be turned from ⁵⁄₄ straight-grained hard maple that I already had.

Parts

I began with the intention of building nine, rather than eight, chairs so that if there was a problem with one, I could substitute that extra copy. Too, if everything went perfectly and I ended up with nine, I would have a chair that I could keep as a sample to give other customers an idea of what chairs built from figured woods looked like.

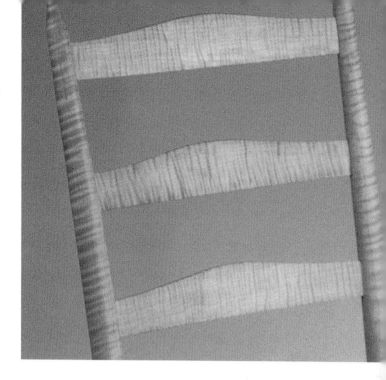

I knew that I would be dealing with a large number of very similar but still different parts. For example, to make this set of nine chairs, I would need 63 side rungs. (The extra seven are the lower back rungs, which are the same length as the six side rungs on each chair.) Eighteen of those would be seat rungs, which meant they would be turned from straight-grained hard maple, rather than the curly red maple I would be using for the other side rungs. Also, I would need 27 front rungs, nine of which would be seat rungs and turned from hard maple.

To avoid confusion at glue-up, it was imperative that I keep all these parts segregated.

I find it is easy to keep the rungs separate in a series of buckets, each designated for a different type of rung. Each chair-maker may have his own system that works well for him. For instance, Charles Harvey, of Berea, Kentucky, uses color coding to differentiate the rungs in his rung kiln.

Although there would be 27 slats in these chairs, they would all be identical and would require no differentiation. Posts, however, were another matter. These would be turned to three different

Turning blanks are stacked on the right. Turned, tenoned, and sanded rungs are stored in buckets until they're needed at assembly. Steam-bent slats are curled around the black bucket, while band-sawn and sanded (but unbent) slats are leaning against the white bucket.

shapes: back posts, front posts for armchairs, and front posts for side chairs. And each of these different shapes would be divided equally into groups of right posts and groups of left posts. The different shapes can be distinguished at a glance, but the difference between a right post and a left post is not so easily seen.

Unlike the rungs, the posts won't fit comfortably in buckets, so in this instance I borrowed Charles's system and color-coded the end grain of the posts with magic markers, one color for right and another for left.

Speaking as someone who is genetically inclined to disorder, some system of parts organization is essential when planning a production run in the small shop. The particular job, the shop, and the craftsman determines what system of organization might work best. My solutions may apply only to chair jobs done in my shop, but I believe that the principle of careful parts organization applies to any shop making multiple copies.

Moisture

Unlike casework, chair-making poses the complication of moisture management. When I'm building a single chair, moisture management is relatively straightforward. After baking thoroughly air-dried rung stock in the oven at 200 degrees F (93 degrees C) for a couple of hours, I turn the rungs and size the tenons. These are then set aside.

Posts are turned from stock in the 20-percent moisture range, with fresh-sawn surfaces damp but not wet. After the posts have been turned and marked, they are taken immediately to the drill press, and front and back rung mortises are bored. Slat mortises are then chopped out by hand.

Once cut, mortises dry very quickly. I've learned that once a mortise is cut, the chair must be assembled. Every hour that a mortised post sits in a heated shop reduces the amount of post shrinkage that can be expected on the rung tenon—and may also require that the tenons be resized to fit the smaller mortises. (If I'm building a chair with bent back posts, I will violate this rule. I drill the mortises for the back rungs prior to bending the posts. Then, to retard drying in the mortises, I dribble water in the mortises and wrap them with tape.)

As soon as the mortises have been cut, I check the size of the rung tenons. If, because they have been sitting in the shop for several days, they have absorbed enough moisture to increase in diameter, I put them in the oven again. The chair is then assembled in stages—front and back ladder first, then, after drilling side rung mortises, the chair itself—pressing the slightly oversized tenons into the rung mortises with a pipe clamp.

However, when working with a large number of chairs, this process must be modified. I begin with the chair rungs, ripping all the turning blanks from ¾ stock and centering them for the lathe. These are then taken to the oven in batches no larger than I can turn by the end of that workday. After they are turned, tenoned, and sanded, they are placed in appropriately marked buckets. After all the rungs have been turned, I direct my attention to the posts.

Ideally, these would be done one chair at a time, but in order to make better use of machine setups, I deal with them all at once, ripping out all the stock on the table saw, then centering it, mounting it in the lathe and turning it. Some moisture is lost because even though the mortises aren't cut until the day of assembly, the turned posts may sit around the shop for a week or more.

I recognize the imperfections in my system, but what I'm looking for is a compromise between the needs of moisture management and the efficient use of tool setups.

Assembly

When ready, I assemble one chair at a time, placing the rungs in the oven for a final round of drying and then, while that's taking place, cutting the mortises for the first chair. After that chair has been completely assembled, I put the next batch of rungs in the oven and cut the mortises for the second chair. Working in this manner, I can assemble three side chairs in a day's time.

Final assembly is intoxicating. The shop is quiet. The radio plays softly. I lay out finished parts— back ladder, front ladder, side rungs, arms—on an old quilt. I spread glue on each tenon and in each mortise. I position the rung tenons. With a pipe clamp, each is driven into its mortise.

Then something happens that I still find remarkable—even after assembling more than two hundred chairs in my shop. As the pipe clamps bring parts together, as the tenons are seated in their mortises, the chair begins to assume its characteristic shape. Ladders, rungs, and arms move, by jerking fits and starts, into alignment. The chair's four feet come to rest purposefully on the benchtop. I rotate the chair in my hands, and, as I wash away dribbles of glue, I feel and see that it is tight, square, and whole.

135

GALLERY OF CHAIRS

▲▽▲▽▲▽▲▽▲▽▲▽▲▽▲▽▲▽▲▽▲▽▲▽▲▽▲▽▲▽▲▽▲▽▲▽▲▽

I feel very lucky to be able to include the following photos of contemporary American chairs, each of which provides an imaginative solution to the problem of providing us with places to sit. Enjoy the feast.

—Kerry Pierce

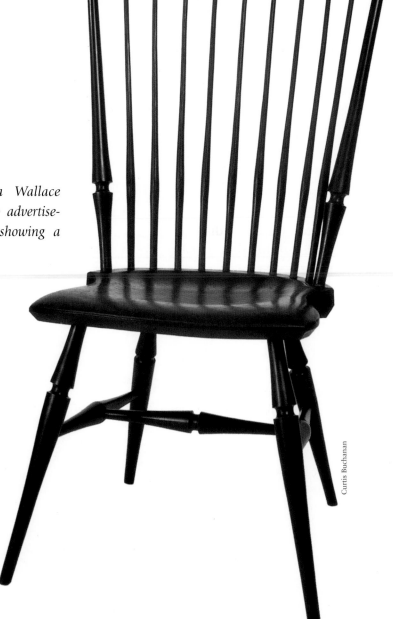

Curtis Buchanan

Jonesborough, Tennessee

"My influences came from a Wallace Nutting piece and from a photo advertisement for the Primrose School showing a chair built by West Lowe."

"Patra's Chair"

Curtis Buchanan

Jerry Anthony

"Continuous Arm Lenox Chair"

Jerry Anthony

"Lenox Settee"

Joe Graham
Jefferson, Ohio

"The beauty of the chair-making tradition is the capacity for individual expression that results from the skillful manipulation of hand-held tools."

In addition to making his own chairs, Graham teaches his craft in workshops held near his rural Jefferson, Ohio, home.

Jerry Anthony

"Writing Arm Lenox Chair"

137

"Dining Chair"

"Rocking Chair"

Owen Rein
Mountain View, Arkansas

"The lines of the grain in the wood follow the lines of the chair. Variations in the grain reveal themselves but still follow those lines."

138

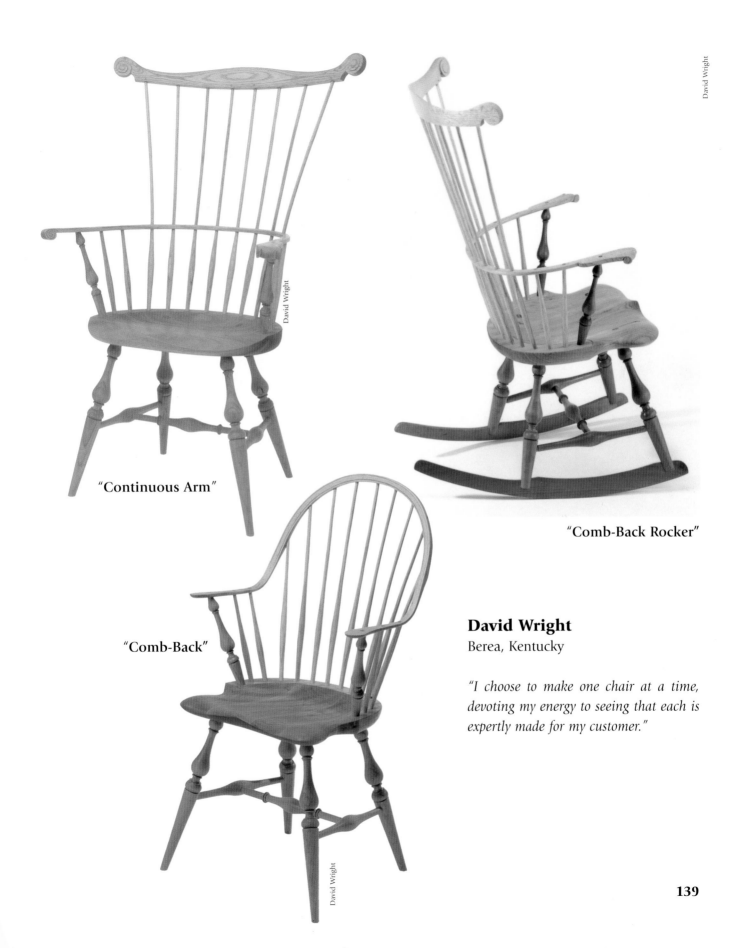

"Continuous Arm"

"Comb-Back Rocker"

"Comb-Back"

David Wright
Berea, Kentucky

"I choose to make one chair at a time, devoting my energy to seeing that each is expertly made for my customer."

139

"Fan Back with Upholstered Seat"

Brian Boggs

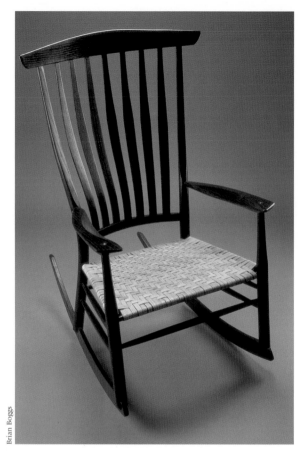

Brian Boggs

"Ebonized Fan Back Rocker"

Brian Boggs
Berea, Kentucky

"I work primarily in cherry, hickory, white oak or red oak. Ash, maple or walnut are also available. Most of my chair seats are woven from hickory bark, but I will also weave seats from cotton Shaker tape."

140

Brian Boggs

"Fan Back Settee"

"Woven Back Rocker"

Brian Boggs

141

"Sunflower Chair"

William Locke

West Roxbury, Massachusetts

"Langley Boardman, who designed the arm-chair, worked in Portsmouth, New Hampshire, during the late eighteenth and ealry nineteenth centuries."

"Armchair"

INDEX

▲▽

METRIC CONVERSION ▲▼▲▼▲▼▲▼▲▼▲▼▲▼▲▼▲▼▲▼▲▼▲▼▲▼

Foot and Inch Conversions

1 inch = 25.4mm
1 foot = 304.8mm

Metric Conversions

1 mm = 0.039 inch
1 m = 3.28 feet

mm = millimeter
cm = centimeter
m = meter

inches	mm	cm	inches	cm	inches	cm
1/8	3	0.3	9	22.9	30	76.2
1/4	6	0.6	10	25.4	31	78.7
3/8	10	1.0	11	27.9	32	81.3
1/2	13	1.3	12	30.5	33	83.8
5/8	16	1.6	13	33.0	34	86.4
3/4	19	1.9	14	35.6	35	88.9
7/8	22	2.2	15	38.1	36	91.4
1	25	2.5	16	40.6	37	94.0
1 1/4	32	3.2	17	43.2	38	96.6
1 1/2	38	3.8	18	45.7	39	99.1
1 3/4	44	4.4	19	48.3	40	101.6
2	51	5.1	20	50.8	41	104.1
2 1/2	64	6.4	21	53.3	42	106.7
3	76	7.6	22	55.9	43	109.2
3 1/2	89	8.9	23	58.4	44	111.8
4	102	10.2	24	61.0	45	114.3
4 1/2	114	11.4	25	63.5	46	116.8
5	127	12.7	26	66.0	47	119.4
6	152	15.2	27	68.6	48	121.9
7	178	17.8	28	71.1	49	124.5
8	203	20.3	29	73.7	50	127.0